THE
EVERYTHING®

PARENT'S GUIDE TO
COMMON CORE ELA: GRADES K–5

Dear Reader,

I am happy that you have picked up this book to learn more about the Common Core ELA (English language arts) Standards. This is an exciting time in education as we are in the implementation stages of these new standards. The standards provide a roadmap to help you prepare your kids for college and career success. The focus is on providing a quality education that is forward focused on the demands of college and the workplace. I am excited to partner with you as we take a closer look at the standards and the new demands they require for student learning. We will begin by looking at the development of the standards and the rationale behind having a national curriculum. We will also look at the anchor standards and the implications they have in preparing kids for college and the workplace. Finally, we will focus on the skills for each grade level and provide activities you can use to reinforce them at home. I know you will enjoy reading the book and learning more about the Common Core ELA Standards.

Dr. Felicia Durden

Welcome to the EVERYTHING® Series!

These handy, accessible books give you all you need to tackle a difficult project, gain a new hobby, comprehend a fascinating topic, prepare for an exam, or even brush up on something you learned back in school but have since forgotten.

You can choose to read an Everything® book from cover to cover or just pick out the information you want from our four useful boxes: e-questions, e-facts, e-alerts, and e-ssentials. We give you everything you need to know on the subject, but throw in a lot of fun stuff along the way, too.

We now have more than 400 Everything® books in print, spanning such wide-ranging categories as weddings, pregnancy, cooking, music instruction, foreign language, crafts, pets, New Age, and so much more. When you're done reading them all, you can finally say you know Everything®!

PUBLISHER Karen Cooper

MANAGING EDITOR, EVERYTHING® SERIES Lisa Laing

COPY CHIEF Casey Ebert

ASSISTANT PRODUCTION EDITOR Alex Guarco

ACQUISITIONS EDITOR Hillary Thompson

SENIOR DEVELOPMENT EDITOR Brett Palana-Shanahan

EVERYTHING® SERIES COVER DESIGNER Erin Alexander

Visit the entire Everything® series at *www.everything.com*

THE EVERYTHING®

PARENT'S GUIDE TO
Common Core ELA: Grades K–5

Understand the new English standards to
help your child learn and succeed

Felicia Durden, EdD

Aadamsmedia
Avon, Massachusetts

*To my loving family, I could not have accomplished this without
your love and support. Thank you Agu for your belief in me. Thank
you Caleb for being the reason I work so hard. Thank you to my
parents Virgil and Nevida. Your encouragement throughout the
years paved the way for my love of learning.*

An Everything® Series Book.
Everything® and everything.com® are registered trademarks of F+W Media, Inc.

Published by
Adams Media, a division of F+W Media, Inc.
57 Littlefield Street, Avon, MA 02322. U.S.A.
www.adamsmedia.com

ISBN 10: 1-4405-9056-7
ISBN 13: 978-1-4405-9056-6
eISBN 10: 1-4405-9057-5
eISBN 13: 978-1-4405-9057-3

Printed in the United States of America.

10   9   8   7   6   5   4   3   2   1

Interior illustrations by Eric Andrews.

*This book is available at quantity discounts for bulk purchases.
For information, please call 1-800-289-0963.*

Contents

Introduction

THERE HAS ALWAYS BEEN an ebb and flow in the field of education. The paradigm shifts that have occurred in education since the founding of our nation have served to ensure that all children, regardless of background, receive a quality education. The basic premise of the American education system is to provide equal access to education for all learners, and accessible educational systems are the cornerstone of our nation. As such, our schools provide children with the basic skills needed to navigate the world.

The idea of a national curriculum has been around even before I began my teaching career over sixteen years ago. Proponents believed that establishing a set of guidelines that determine the required educational skills at each grade level would help ensure a standardized and more equitable system.

The developers of the Common Core standards have taken the idea of equity to include providing students with the skills needed to be college and career ready (CCR). The authors of the Common Core took the necessary skills for college and career readiness, and from there, mapped backgrounds to show where the student should be by the end of high school. This focus on mapping educational standards from kindergarten to college has gained a lot of support, as colleges and workplace managers understand that many of our kids have not been prepared to meet proficiency standards for college and the workforce. The idea of rigor and relevance is a very important focus of the Common Core English language arts (ELA) standards. The standards require a higher cognitive awareness. This means that the rigor of the standards requires students to not just use basic recall to answer questions about the texts they read; instead, they have to read and synthesize information to form ideas and make inferences from the text. This level of rigor increases as students move through the grades. In the primary grade levels (K–2), a lot of teacher support is provided to teach students to think about what they are reading and form opinions based on information in the text. As students get into higher grade levels (3–5), they begin to independently perform these tasks. You will hear the word *rigor* continually as we move into the Common Core era. Keep in mind that rigor does not mean giving kids things that are difficult so they struggle. Rigor is based on the depth of knowledge required for the skill. In the opening paragraph we talked about paradigm shifts. For years educators have used Bloom's Taxonomy, a framework for teachers to use to focus on higher-order thinking, to determine the level of understanding/rigor of a task.

Bloom's Taxonomy of learning includes knowledge, comprehension, application, analysis, synthesis, and evaluation. The lowest level on Bloom's Taxonomy is knowledge, which includes basic rote memory skills—something the Common Core is steering students away from. The highest level, evaluation, focuses on making judgments of inferences about content.

The tool we are now using to determine rigor for the Common Core is Webb's Depth of Knowledge. There are four levels in Webb's Depth of Knowledge:

Level 1 (Recall)
Level 2 (Skill/Concept)
Level 3 (Strategic Thinking)
Level 4 (Extended Thinking)

Rigor is determined by the tasks that students are asked to complete. A lower-level task would be to define a noun or verb. At level 4, an example would be to analyze how verbs were used to convey tone in a story.

Making content relevant is also an important dimension to the Common Core ELA standards. Students are learning the importance of being a competent reader and writer. The tasks that students perform in class will be used to prepare them for college and the workplace. Building this connection to the real world allows your child to understand the importance of his learning and how he can hone those skills to prepare himself to be successful in life. We have always known how important it is for students to understand the reason they are learning something. The standards do this by providing a staircase of complexity of tasks that are relevant to the types of situations and tasks students will perform in the workplace and in college.

This book will provide a simplified view of the Common Core ELA standards. We will discuss the standards and provide activities you can use at home to help prepare your child for the demands of the Common Core ELA standards. Each chapter will include hands-on activities and ideas you can try with your child. This no-nonsense guide to the ELA standards will be a resource you can refer to as you are working with your child and gaining further understanding of the standards. I look forward to learning along with you as we explore the Common Core ELA standards together.

CHAPTER 1

Overview of the Common Core State Standards

In recent years there has been a strong push to standardize what is taught in America's classrooms. In the past what students were learning in one state was often very different than what students were learning in another state. The Common Core standards are an effort to provide learning consistency across the nation. The premise behind this movement is to ensure all students have access to a rigorous curriculum that promotes college and career readiness. It does so by providing standards that build on one another from one grade level to the next. This chapter provides an overview of the Common Core ELA (English language arts) standards. It presents the development of the ELA standards and their primary focus. This chapter also covers strategies you can use at home to help your child.

What Are the Common Core Standards?

The Common Core standards are a set of educational measurements for students in kindergarten through high school. Standards have always been a part of schooling. Standards refer to the content and curriculum that is taught in classrooms each day. Traditionally, each state has had its own set of standards and methods for teaching students. In recent years there has been a push to set national standards in schools across the nation. This would mean that, for example, a student in the first grade in one state would be taught the same standards as a student in first grade in another state. By ensuring that students across America are being taught using the same standards, state-by-state comparisons can be aligned so that all students in America can be tested using the same standards of learning.

ESSENTIAL

The name Common Core State Standards also has significance. The term *common* refers to a set of standards that are common across the United States. The term *core* refers to the fundamental and essential core standards that will prepare kids for college and career. The term *state* refers to the fact that the standards were developed in cooperation with governors from each state. And finally, the term *standards* refers to the agreed-upon standards of learning for each grade level.

How Did We Get Here?

The Common Core standards started with two organizations in Washington, D.C. The two organizations are the National Governors Association Center for Best Practices (NGA) and the Council of Chief State School Officers (CCSSO). The National Governors Association was founded in 1908 and is a bipartisan organization. The members include the current governors from all fifty states and the territories of American Samoa, Guam, Northern Mariana Islands, Puerto Rico, and the U.S. Virgin Islands. In 2007 Janet Napolitano, then the serving chair of the NGA, discussed the need to ensure that American children were ready to compete globally. This discussion spearheaded what we now know as the Common Core State Standards Initiative.

FACT

The intent of the Common Core standards is to provide a set of rigorous, high-expectation standards that prepare our kids to be college and career ready. These standards provide a roadmap for schools on what is to be taught at each grade level in an effort to achieve this goal.

The Common Core standards provide clear and consistent expectations regarding what students need to know by the end of each grade level. They are built on a staircase of difficulty, meaning that the standards increase in complexity as students move from one grade to the next. The writers of the Common Core aimed to provide clear transitions from grade to grade so that students can confidently meet the challenges of the subsequent grades. The subject areas of the standards include math and English language arts (ELA) (for all grade levels), and literacy in history/social studies, science, and technical subjects (for grades 6–12):

- **Math:** The math standards focus on problem solving and precision. These standards follow a staircase of difficulty and take students from one grade to the next with connected standards that build upon one another.
- **English Language Arts (ELA):** The ELA standards build foundational skills that prepare children to read complex texts with confidence. This includes the ability to read grade-level text fluently.
- **History/Social Studies, Science, and Technical Subjects:** The literacy standards for history/social studies, science, and technical subjects provide guidance on how to read technical texts and understand the text structures for students in grades 6–12.

This book explores the Common Core State Standards for English language arts (most commonly referred to as the Common Core ELA standards), the impact the standards will have on classroom instruction, and how you, as a parent, can help your child with these standards.

A Nation at Risk

For decades America had been falling behind other countries in academic achievement. Further, despite federal mandates like the No Child Left Behind Act (NCLB) of 2001, the achievement gap between students from low socioeconomic backgrounds and those from high socioeconomic backgrounds was not being bridged. One of the biggest "wake-up calls" for the educational system came in 1983 with the U.S. Department of Education's release of the report *A Nation at Risk*, which revealed the socioeconomic educational achievement gap. The report, which was commissioned by then President Ronald Reagan to assess the current state of schools, indicated that the American educational system was in crisis due to low performance and inadequate student achievement. The conclusions from the report were clear: American students were not prepared to face the challenges of a modern society as they were lacking the necessary skills to think critically and read. From the report findings, legislators were encouraged to increase measures to meet the needs of all learners. After the report was released, educational funding increased by more than 30 percent, and forty-seven states passed major educational reform bills. *A Nation at Risk* was a call to action, and proponents noted that it was a propelling element in the public demand for change in the educational system.

The History of American Education

Around 1635, as public schools were being established, a debate arose among the church leadership, private school advocates, and public school proponents. Each group had a conflicting viewpoint regarding the establishment of a free and public education system. Church leaders and private school advocates argued that their vested interests would not be taken into account if a free public education system existed. Others maintained that the idea of having a free common school could not be a reality because schools should be reserved for the elite and those with leisure time. They proposed that schooling should be reserved for gentry and should not include the poor.

FACT

Boston Latin School is the oldest public school in America. It was founded in 1635.

In order to understand the complexities of America's schools, it is important to understand the historical roots of the current educational system. The formal education system began in the 1840s when the common school model was introduced. Common schools established publicly funded elementary schools that offered a basic education, which included a reading, writing, and arithmetic curriculum. The schools were called "common" because they were open to children from all socioeconomic classes. However, enslaved African American children in Southern states were prohibited from attending schools until after the Civil War when slavery was abolished.

Finally, in 1852, legislators accepted the idea of free public schools and followed specific steps to get the current model of free, public, compensatory education implemented. First, they permitted residents to organize local school districts; second, they encouraged but did not require establishing school districts, electing school boards, and levying taxes to support schools; finally, they made common schools compulsory by mandating the establishment of districts and election boards and raising taxes to support them. With the establishment of free common schools, a compelling idea emerged: America could provide a free education for all regardless of race and class.

College Readiness

Although students from around the world come to American universities and colleges prepared for college-level learning, there seems to be a problem in preparing American children to meet the demands of college. In 2010 ACT, Inc. (a company best known for creating the ACT college readiness assessment test) published a report called *A First Look at the Common Core and College and Career Readiness*. In it, ACT revealed that American kids overall were not ready for the demands of the Common Core standards. Indeed, each year our colleges are filled with students in developmental reading, writing, and math courses. Colleges and universities scramble each year to create more sessions of remedial math and writing courses because so many students do not pass the entrance exams to grant placement in English 101 or college-level mathematics. Many of these students are bright but need to learn how to reason and write using text-based evidence that is required of college-level writers.

Political and business leaders, educators, and parents alike are troubled by the problem of a child graduating from high school and yet not be capable of going right into college-level material. This is a big part of why the focus on college and career readiness, beginning in kindergarten, is a major part of the Common Core standards development.

Career Readiness

Another goal of the Common Core standards is to prepare students to be career ready. Companies want entry-level employees to enter the workforce who can think critically, work well in groups, think on their feet, multitask, and complete training programs efficiently and effectively. As with colleges, companies are also finding that students who enter the workforce after high school graduation are not prepared to contribute effectively in the workplace. Companies are finding that they need to provide high school graduates with training and other supports to remediate skills that these young adults should already possess. The goal of the Common Core standards is to decrease those numbers and better prepare our kids for the challenges of entry-level careers, freshman-level college courses, and workforce training programs.

What Is the Instructional Aim of the Common Core ELA Standards?

The authors of the Common Core standards have tried to provide a set of standards that will level the playing field for American kids to compete nationally. To achieve this aim, teachers across America are being trained on how to implement these standards into their classrooms.

QUESTION

How do American students compare to students around the world? By leveling the playing field, the Common Core State Standards help ensure that American kids are able to compete globally. A short video produced by CTB/McGraw-Hill provides a great explanation of how our kids are competing with other nations: *www.youtube.com/watch?v=JOdvdPnFXTQ.*

As parents, we all want the best for our kids. And we want all of our children to achieve at high levels. The Common Core standards are designed to support this desire and ensure that all students receive instruction that is aligned to a set of standards that will prepare them for decades to come. In reality, your kids may be competing for jobs that have not even been invented yet. In fact, in the next few years many jobs will become obsolete while new jobs that have not even been imagined will come into existence. The Common Core standards were developed to ready our kids for these very real workplace demands, wherever in the globe these jobs may be.

What Does This Mean for Your Child's Classroom?

The Common Core standards determine what is taught in the classrooms across America. With more rigorous expectations for learning, classroom instruction will shift from being a teacher-centered environment to one in which students are at the center. Students will be required to analyze content and develop ideas from their reading. Teachers will move from product-based learning to deeper learning and evaluation of topics.

As a parent, you may notice that your child is asked to read texts that are more complex than what you might expect, and that the writing tasks she completes will be based on providing evidence from the text rather than just offering an opinion on a topic. You may also notice that your child is reading fiction and nonfiction texts about the same subject while she is building her knowledge base and forming opinions from her reading. Your child may read a story about a particular topic, watch a video about the same topic, and read an article on the topic as well. She may then be asked to write an essay discussing how the three sources differed and what they had in common. This is certainly a different process than the typical prompt-based writing that has been in place for many years. Regurgitating facts will no longer be the norm, and students will now have to build understanding of historical topics.

Another noted change in classroom practice will be that teachers will teach with resources that are relevant and timely. The Common Core standards have a significant focus on using multimedia resources and integrating technology. The Common Core assessments are computer based, thus teachers will begin to implement more technology into the curriculum, and students will be conducting Internet research and typing essays at a much earlier age.

Helping Your Child Learn with the Common Core Standards

The Common Core standards provide building blocks to prepare our kids for the next generation and beyond. The standards promote analysis, precision, and flexibility. Students will be required to analyze topics from different points of view, synthesize information with precision and provide a succinct summary, and have the ability to be flexible enough to work across content areas to complete work tasks.

This book focuses on strategies for you to use at home to help support your child with the increased demands of the Common Core ELA standards. Some strategies this book will focus on include ways to engage your child in reading multiple texts on a subject to gain understanding, ideas on how to use writing as a way to enhance reading comprehension, and how to use graphic organizers to help with reading and writing.

CHAPTER 2

Instructional Shifts

The Common Core ELA standards support six key instructional shifts. These shifts represent the instructional changes that the standards require in your child's classroom. The authors of the Common Core use the term *instructional shift* because this term represents a change in the way teachers present information in the classroom, and a shift in what is expected of each child. This chapter discusses the six shifts and the impact they have in the classroom.

What Is an Instructional Shift?

Think of this shift as an adjustment in how information is presented in the classroom. Shifts will be evident in the way teachers present information (including having more group work and teaching multiple skills at one time) and the level of expectation they will demand of students, such as reading more challenging texts and then analyzing those texts to determine theme.

The fundamental change in instruction is how teachers teach rather than what they are teaching. Common Core ELA standards require that teachers "shift" their focus from memorization and fact-finding to discovery and connected learning. The days of remembering basic math facts and random historical dates are gone; they are being replaced with students having to actually delve into a subject and come up with clarified understandings of skills and events.

Students who engage in activities where they connect their learning to their personal experiences of the real world are more likely to retain the information than when they rely on memorizing facts and dates.

The Common Core ELA standards support six instructional shifts. These six shifts in English language arts are increased reading of informational text, increased text complexity, increased academic vocabulary, text-based answers, increased writing from sources, and literary instruction in all content areas.

Shift 1: Increased Reading of Informational Text

The first change in classroom practice that the Common Core ELA standards require is an increased use of informational, nonfiction texts. Typically, students in the primary grades (students in kindergarten through fifth grade) read stories, poetry, and other fictional texts. This is especially true in kindergarten and first grade classrooms. Students in these classrooms can be found reading storybooks and rehearsing chants and rhymes as they build their knowledge of words.

Fiction is a wonderful way to engage children in wordplay and to expose them to the structure of story (characters, setting, events, and so forth). Yet, it is also just as important for children in these grade levels to have access to informational text and nonfiction so they can develop an appreciation for and become acquainted with the structures of these types of material. The goal of the Common Core ELA standards is to intentionally expose children to these diverse text types starting in kindergarten.

50/50 Split

Shift 1 supports exposing students to more informational text starting in kindergarten. In fact, Common Core calls for a 50/50 split of the teaching of fictional or literary text and nonfiction text for students in grades kindergarten through fifth grade. This means that your child will be reading fiction and informational or nonfiction texts during his reading instruction. This is a change, because for years most primary reading textbooks had a majority of fictional texts for students to read.

ESSENTIAL

You may wonder why there is now an emphasis on informational text and nonfiction. The fact is, informational text or nonfiction represents most of the reading required in college and the workplace. Most college textbooks, product manuals, and training materials in the workplace are informational. Thus, teaching children how to read these materials and to be comfortable comprehending them is important.

The Common Core calls for a 50/50 split in kindergarten–grade 5; 60/40 in grades 6–8; and 70/30 in grades 9–12:

GRADES K–5
- 50/50: Students are given a proportional split of fiction and nonfiction. This means that teachers should include a balanced amount of fiction and nonfiction in their classroom teaching.

GRADES 6–8

- 60/40: Students are given a 60 percent exposure to nonfiction and 40 percent to fiction. This standard requires that students use informational/nonfiction texts in their non-literature content blocks including math, science, and social studies.

GRADES 9–12

- 70/30: High school students are given a 70 percent exposure to nonfiction with only a 30 percent exposure to fiction. This requires that teachers in content areas like math, science, and social studies include informational/nonfiction texts in their classroom lessons.

Learning to Read and Reading to Learn

In grade 4 and beyond students typically focus more on reading to learn than on developing reading skills or learning to read. These students should be reading texts at their grade level independently so that they may be ready for the demands of standards and their increased complexity. It is important to know that your child has a greater exposure to informational text as she moves up in grade levels because it allows you to support learning beyond the classroom. For example, you can make age-appropriate informational texts easily available around the home. To accomplish this, you could subscribe to children's science, sports, or environmental magazines or have informational texts such as science magazines, science booklets, history books, and informational pamphlets on topics of interest, to name a few. Having these resources at home will encourage your child to make quick reads on information of interest.

ESSENTIAL

Here is a list of magazines that you can consider making available to your children: *Ranger Rick, Sports Illustrated Kids, Time For Kids, National Geographic Kids, Wild Animal Baby,* and *Big Backyard.* Your local library probably already subscribes to most of these magazines and many others.

Prior to the Common Core ELA standards, students in grades K–2 were required to read little nonfiction; many schools had placed more of an emphasis on narrative and fictional texts. This was evident because in state assessments students were doing well on the fictional texts. However, these students were not doing as well on standardized tests when reading informational, nonfictional text types. Many students scored significantly lower on test items that were related to nonfiction texts.

What Will Shift 1 Look Like in the Classroom?

When developing the standards, the Common Core authors looked at the NAEP standards. (NAEP stands for the National Assessment of Educational Progress.) The NAEP had found that the amount of informational text students were using was not enough to adequately prepare them for the demands of college and career. The authors of the Common Core then developed standards to remedy this problem.

ESSENTIAL

The NAEP is the largest assessment given nationally to determine how American students are doing in comparison to one another. The data received from the NAEP are used to determine national trends. The results from the NAEP are used in The Nation's Report Card (see *www.nationsreportcard.gov*).

Each year the NAEP assessment is administered to students throughout the nation. For years, this has served as the only national assessment that has been used across all fifty states. The results from the NAEP were pivotal in determining which areas students were struggling in.

So what will this mean for classroom shifts? The main shift you will notice in the classroom is that teachers will be teaching children how to read nonfictional text. Students now are expected to read nonfiction and informational texts and discuss the vocabulary, themes, and key concepts these texts focus on. This is quite different from reading a fictional story and then talking about the characters, plot, setting, and so forth.

How did your state do on the 2013 NAEP reading assessment? Check out your state's results on the 2013 reading test here: *https:// nces.ed.gov/nationsreportcard/reading/stateassessment.aspx.*

Reading: Informational Text

The Common Core standards additionally support the idea that teachers of all subject matters have the responsibility of teaching reading, not just the English teacher. Children will now see informational texts in science and social studies contexts, meaning they will be reading texts related to science and social studies and applying their comprehension skills to determine key ideas and meaning.

As a result of this shift, students will be able to learn more about the world around them. Informational text structures can be difficult for many kids to understand, so teachers have to teach students *how* to read informational text and understand the text structures. Reading nonfiction is quite different from reading fiction; think about your purpose when reading the newspaper versus reading a novel. Preparing kids to read articles, procedures, pamphlets, and other informational text is important for students as they move into college and career. This shift will ensure that these important literary skills are taught starting in kindergarten. So be prepared, because you can expect to see a lot of emphasis on informational text in the coming years.

Shift 2: Text Complexity

Another important shift that the Common Core standards promote is an increase in text complexity. "Reading Between the Lines," a 2006 report released by ACT, notes that when students didn't achieve benchmark scores on the ACT standardized test, their struggles had more to do with their comprehension of complex passages and less to do with using the specific skills called for by the questions. This shows that what students are able to read, in terms of complexity, is at least as important as what they can do with what they read. Further, this means that a student's inability to complete a reading task is related to the complexity of the text itself.

FACT

Reading between the lines refers to the ability to make inferences about meaning by analyzing texts and going beyond the plot and characters. This prepares students for advanced comprehension skills that require purposeful reading to draw meaning from the unstated.

What Determines Text Complexity?

The Common Core standards evaluate a text's complexity based on three components: quantitative measures, qualitative measures, and reader and task considerations.

- *Quantitative* refers to the readability of the text. To determine this, schools could use a text's Lexile score. The Lexile score is based on the word length and sentence length. (Most often, computers are used to determine a Lexile score based on these measures.) This measure cannot be used alone, however, because some complex works may have low Lexile scores because they feature shorter words and sentences.
- *Qualitative* refers to the level of meaning. This includes looking at the language used, conventions, and the demands of knowledge required to understand the text. Think about science texts you have read. They often use high-level vocabulary and demand that the reader has the ability to comprehend complex ideas.
- *Reader and task considerations* are concerned with the intent of the text and the task it requires of the student. It is measured by determining the prior knowledge necessary for the student to understand the text. This means it depends on the student and what the teacher asks him to do with a text. For example, a text with a low Lexile level can be complex if a student has limited prior knowledge. Think about trying to read the manual on your DVD player. The text itself is not difficult, but understanding what you are required to do to get the device connected can require some complex understanding.

Textbooks and Text Complexity

Over the past few decades, textbooks in America have continually decreased in their level of difficulty. There has been a decline in sentence length and vocabulary since the 1960s. This was due in part to an effort to ensure that all students could access the content. However, this decline has contributed to students being unprepared to tackle college-level texts. The United States currently has a 350 Lexile gap between the difficulty of the texts used at the end of high school and the texts used at entry-level college. This means that high school students are not reading texts at a high enough Lexile range to be prepared for reading college-level texts. The problem is that the kindergarten–grade 12 Lexile levels have decreased over the last half century, while the college and workplace-training materials have retained and even increased their Lexile levels over this same period.

The Common Core readjustment of the text complexity requires a two-to-three-year jump in Lexile levels. This is a challenge for many students because they have to learn strategies to read complex texts independently without frustration. This offers a great opportunity for kids to struggle with text in the classroom so the teacher can offer support and strategies to help children find ways to confidently read complex texts by using strategies to comprehend the meaning of the text.

Chunking and Scaffolding

Teachers have typically chunked, scaffolded, or leveled down complex texts so that students can understand the context of the information. This chunking or scaffolding refers to breaking the tasks down into steps that are less intimidating for students. This would include providing teacher support when reading an unfamiliar word or providing a text at a lower Lexile level. Traditionally, teachers have used methods such as giving the student graphics to help understand the key themes, reading the text aloud, and connecting the text to background knowledge in an effort to make complex texts easier for students to understand.

The authors of the Common Core do not advocate for *not* providing support, but they do advocate that teachers allow kids to struggle with complex texts while guiding the students on which strategies to use. The terms *with guidance* and *support* are used continually in the Common Core standards.

The following chart shows the new Lexile levels. As you can see, the ranges have increased significantly in each grade.

TEXT COMPLEXITY AND ASSOCIATED LEXILE RANGES		
Grade-Level Band	**Old Lexile Ranges**	**New Lexile Ranges**
K–1	N/A	N/A
2–3	450–725	450–790
4–5	645–845	770–980
6–8	860–1010	955–1155
9–10	960–1115	1080–1305
11–CCR	1070–1220	1215–1355
Table adapted from lexile.com		

What Will Instructional Shift 2 Look Like in the Classroom?

Instructional shift 2 focuses on increasing the Lexile levels for all grade levels. This will impact the classroom by requiring students to read these more complex grade-level texts. The Common Core ELA standard that relates to this instructional shift in reading is standard 10. Reading standard

10 focuses on a student's ability to read complex texts at and above grade-level bands. Grade-level bands refer to the grade levels that are associated with the Lexile levels. The grade-bands are K–1, 2–3, and 4–5. This is illustrated in the chart in the previous section. The Common Core has raised those grade-level bands so students will be exposed to more complex texts at their grade level. The Common Core standards note that support and scaffolding are needed as students go across the grade-level bands. That support and scaffolding may come in the form of using templates, teacher coaching, or teacher modeling. Another practice that the Common Core ELA supports is having children listen to classic literature. Teachers will read classic literature aloud. Some of the classic stories that the Common Core lists for kindergarten read aloud include *The Wonderful Wizard of Oz* by L. Frank Baum, *Little House in the Big Woods* by Laura Ingalls Wilder, and *Mr. Popper's Penguins* by Richard and Florence Atwater. These are all classic stories that a kindergarten student cannot read aloud, but can listen to for enjoyment. Teachers can also discuss the stories to explore the different themes and key ideas in the text. Appendix B of the Common Core ELA standards has lists of recommended literature for each grade level.

ESSENTIAL

When reading stories aloud with your child take the time to ask questions about the characters, setting, and events. This is a great way to reinforce important comprehension skills.

Shift 3: Academic Vocabulary

The Common Core ELA standards support an increase in the level of academic vocabulary students will be exposed to. Because the Common Core increases text complexity and requires more engagement with informational texts, improvements in academic vocabulary is vitally important to student success. Providing students with vocabulary instruction has always been a fundamental part of education. You may have heard your child's teacher use the terms Tier 1, Tier 2, and Tier 3 when describing vocabulary words:

- **Tier 1** words are basic vocabulary words. These words typically don't have more than one meaning. (Words like *girl*, *boy*, and *book*.)
- **Tier 2** words are those high-impact vocabulary words that cross content areas. They are general academic words. (Words like *justify*, *explain*, and *summarize*.)
- **Tier 3** words are content-specific words. They are words that only relate to the specific subject being taught. (Words like *photosynthesis* and *chromosome*.)

ALERT

Learning vocabulary can be challenging for kids. To help your child store new vocabulary in his long-term memory bank have him use new vocabulary words at any given opportunity. This allows your child to internalize the word and become confident in knowing how to use it.

Vocabulary instruction will continue to be a priority in schools. Comprehension will be impeded if students are not able to comprehend the vocabulary related to the texts they are reading. Think about a time when you were reading a medical article or a technical booklet. Although the words on the page are in English, because of the content-specific vocabulary, often comprehension is impeded.

Shift 4: Text-Based Answers

Another shift that the authors of the Common Core ELA standards want to advance is shift 4, where students provide evidence from text when responding in writing, speaking, and reading. Gone are the days of students writing about their opinions without using the context of the text to support their conclusions.

Students must use evidence from the text in their responses and conclusions. The Common Core standards require that students use the information they learn from their reading to justify their claims. This activity prepares students for college where they will be required to include research findings in their work.

Students in K–5 can demonstrate text-based answering by explaining both the type of evidence they find and the evidence from the text that supports their findings.

Shift 5: Writing from Sources

The fifth shift requires that students use information they find from their research. Students will no longer focus on writing pieces that reflect personal opinion and loosely researched facts. Students are very good at writing about what they know (themselves, family, and friends), but the standards call for more reflective writing that includes key details and events in their narratives.

The standards emphasize research writing. In fact, students as young as kindergarten age are expected to research topics and write about them. This is done with scaffolding and support from adults, but this type of instruction is designed to introduce students to the components and process of independent research writing.

The standards are clear in their expectation for students to include primary and secondary resources in their research pieces. This deeper level of research means students must evaluate sources to determine if they are relevant, and then carefully choose the sources to include in the research report. This is a noted change from the past decade when the typical writing done in schools was narrative writing and opinion pieces. Narrative and opinion writing is no longer prevalent; there is now a focus on research writing that incorporates outside research. This means that students will be required to gather outside resources to include in their writing tasks.

ESSENTIAL

It will be important for students to understand how to value the resources that they include in their writing. In our digital age students are bombarded with information from many resources. They will need to sift through the information to determine what sources of information are most accurate and appropriate for the tasks at hand.

There is one final note to remember about writing from resources: With the shift to a focus on more nonfiction texts, students will be exposed to more technical writing, which incorporates outside research. This instruction is designed to help students increase their ability to shift their writing to include text references.

Shift 6: Literacy Instruction in All Content Areas

With Common Core standards in place, literacy standards are taught in the context of science, social studies, and technical subjects, including math. This is a major shift, especially at the high school level. For years students in math, science, and social studies classes were taught the content of the particular course with little to no instruction on reading strategies. Teachers now use the Common Core standards to help students obtain the skills they need to read informational text. With this expectation, teachers in all content areas work together to determine the skills needed to teach children the concepts of a given subject. As a parent, you can help out at home by talking about literature, math, science, and social studies texts. Helping your child understand the importance of written communication in both fiction and informational texts is a great way to help her internalize the value of this standard. The goal is for your child to be fluent in reading fiction and informational text, and this can only be accomplished if she spends time and effort engaged in the process of learning how to do so.

FACT

A distinct change with the Common Core standards is the notion that all teachers are now responsible for teaching literacy. This includes the math, social studies, science, and technical subject area teachers. This means that your child will be reading in multiple subject areas to support her ability to comprehend texts in different context areas.

A noted difference in the classroom will be more reading and writing in science, social studies, and math classes. I recently saw a group of students writing in their math journals about the formulas they had learned and how they relate to the real world. It was great to see the kids using their writing skills to determine what the key ideas were that they wanted to share and the appropriate vocabulary to clarify meaning.

CHAPTER 3

Breakdown of the ELA Standards

The K–5 Common Core ELA standards are broken down into six sections: Reading: Foundational Skills, Reading: Literature, Reading: Informational Text, Language, Speaking and Listening and Writing. Each of these distinct areas has standards attached to it. The Reading: Foundational Skills standards are found only in grades K–5 and drop off for grades 6 and above. The other five standards, Reading: Literature, Reading: Informational Text, Language, Speaking and Listening, and Writing, are included in ELA for grades 6–12. This chapter discusses the six ELA standards areas for grades K–5, and provides ideas for things you can do at home to support the standards.

Reading: Foundational Skills Standards

The Reading: Foundational Skills standards focus on teaching students how to read. These standards include the foundational phonics, phonemic awareness, and decoding skills that students need to be proficient readers. This includes teaching students about print concepts, the alphabetic principle, phonics, and decoding skills.

QUESTION

Why is phonics instruction important?
The knowledge of letter sounds and their relation to words helps kids easily decode unknown words and quickly read known words. These skills are essential for building comprehension in reading.

The authors of the Common Core have included these very important foundational skills because they are the building blocks students need to become readers. In other words, the Foundational Skills standards are a necessary component of teaching children to read. The standards have increased the rigor in the teaching of reading.

ESSENTIAL

One of the major worries of reading gurus across the nation was that with the focus on comprehension and reading complex texts, teachers may forget the importance of teaching children to read. Without a focus on the Reading: Foundational Skills standards that emphasize teaching students to read, students will not be able to comprehend complex texts as they move up the grade levels.

This leveling up or increased cognitive demand of the Common Core ELA Reading: Foundational Skills standards is important when you think about the demands of increased text complexity, as mentioned in the previous chapter. Students are now required to read at the higher grade-level band by the end of each school year. Once kids are in 3rd grade they are expected to independently read at a 5th grade level, which means that there is no time to waste in teaching kids to read. It is significant to note that the

Reading: Foundational Skills standards discontinue after grade 5. After the 5th grade the focus shifts from teaching children to read to reading to learn by building meaning and arguments from the text. This will be discussed further in the grade-specific chapters.

One last note about the Reading: Foundational Skills standards is that they provide a baseline of what phonics skills should be mastered from one grade level to the next. Ensure that your child's teacher provides you a phonics continuum so you are aware of the instructional sequence your child will follow.

What You Can Do at Home to Help

As a parent you are your child's first teacher. The time spent with your child reading storybooks, singing songs, and talking throughout the years are all experiences that build the foundation for reading. Never underestimate the importance of reading with and to your child. By instilling a love for reading you will impart a major impact on your child's future educational success.

ALERT

Students who spend a minimum of thirty minutes a day reading independently, at an appropriate level (meaning they can understand 85 percent of what they read), experience the most growth in reading. Encourage your child to read daily for at least thirty minutes to help her build her reading skills.

It is now more important than ever that kids come to school prepared to learn to read. A way to help build on these pivotal Reading: Foundational Skills standards is to read with your child. Children can comprehend texts at two to three grade levels above their actual grade. Read classic tales like *Alice's Adventures in Wonderland* and *The Wonderful Wizard of Oz* or any of the books listed on the Common Core text list to your child and ask comprehension questions. Talk about the characters in the story and the events that take place. This is a good way to model the importance of reading to understand and make meaning. Make it a game-like activity so that your child begins to enjoy reading and understands that reading is something that can be done for pleasure.

ESSENTIAL

There is essential research that has found that teaching nursery rhymes helps build phonemic awareness. Phonemic awareness has been found to be a predictor of future reading success.

Another way to build on the Reading: Foundational Skills standards is to play word games with your child. All the rhyming and alliteration that we adults enjoyed as children are also very important to your child's learning. You can do this at home with your child by reciting nursery rhymes and poems. For example, read the following nursery rhymes with your child:

Mary, Mary,
Quite contrary,
How does your garden grow?
With silver bells,
And cockle shells,
And pretty maids all in a row.

Little Miss Muffet
Sat on a tuffet,
Eating her curds and whey;
Along came a spider
Who sat down beside her
And frightened Miss Muffet away.

When reading the nursery rhyme ask your child which two words rhyme. After reading "Mary, Mary, Quite Contrary" explain, for example, that "grow" and "row" are rhyming words because they sound alike. Next, read "Little Miss Muffet" and have your child tell you which words rhyme in the nursery rhyme.

In early literacy teaching, rhyme is an important precursory skill to decoding. Learning to read requires subsequent steps of development, and rhyming is just one of the required skill sets.

FACT

Nursery rhymes have several other purposes in helping children to develop early literacy skills. They allow children to hear new words like "pail" and "fetch." They also typically have a storyline with a beginning, middle, and end, which helps prepare kids for reading storybooks. Finally, they help kids to improve their memory skills. Learning new words, developing a sense of story craft, and building memory skills are all important and valuable skills for the beginning reader.

You can repeat this activity with any rhyming poem or song that you and your child like to recite. Again, make it fun and playful so that your child develops a joy in playing with language. Think about all the TV programs on PBS, like *Sesame Street* and *The Electric Company,* that emphasize wordplay to teach kids sounds in a fun and playful way. These programs often put text and speech bubbles on the television screen to cue children and help them understand that words are sounds that are connected to meaning. As much as possible, practice rhyming with your child to enforce these skills.

Learning the Alphabet and Letter Sounds

Kids who go into kindergarten knowing their letters tend to outperform their peers who do not. They are able to move faster through the concepts and can more quickly go into learning the letter sounds that put them on the road to reading.

Learning the alphabet can be done by breaking it down into three important dimensions. First, you want to start this instruction by having your child know the names of the letters. The best way to do this is to introduce your child to the alphabet song. Second, you should help your child to be able to recognize letters when she sees them in books or in other print sources. You can practice this by asking your child to point to the letter "a," or the letter "c" in a text. Finally, you can help your child learn how to write the letters of the alphabet. Be patient with your child. Letter formation can be quite difficult for kids because they are also developing their fine motor skills.

What do I do if my child is having a hard time learning the letters of the alphabet?
If your child is having trouble learning her letters, try engaging her senses into the process. You can do this by having her make the letters using clay or household items like beans, macaroni, cotton balls, and so forth. Sometimes the motion of creating the letters using tactile methods helps kids internalize the learning and seat it into their long-term memory.

The best rule is to not introduce too much to your child at a time. Many parents are gung ho and, despite very good intentions, overwhelm their children by introducing too many concepts at once. This can be frustrating for your child, which in turn is frustrating for you as a parent. Remember, make it fun, take your time, and celebrate your child's success.

Hearing Sounds

Focus on the alphabet and the letter sounds with young children. Children must first hear the sound to be able to read it. That is why wordplay is an important skill to focus on at home. Continue to sing songs, read poems, and play rhyming games with your child. These are great ways to support the alphabetic principles of letter and sound recognition.

Many fear that the Common Core Reading: Foundational Skills standards are not explicit enough to teach these pivotal reading skills of letter sound recognition and the ability to hear distinct sounds. Rest assured that primary teachers are highly skilled in knowing the importance of the Reading: Foundational Skills and that our schools have a strong focus on early literacy.

Reading: Literature Standards

The Reading: Literature standards focus on the standards that relate to the teaching of fictional texts including poems, stories, and narratives. The Reading: Literature standards focus on the characters, setting, and story elements that teachers have taught for years. The difference in the Common Core standards is the level of understanding that students must possess in terms of making inferences and determining the central meaning of texts.

Because the literature that students will read will be in a higher complexity band, the ability to critically analyze texts to build meaning will be increasingly important. It also will be equally important for students to understand how to make inferences about text meaning by using their life experiences and the text itself as a resource.

Many of the Reading: Literature and Reading: Informational Text standards are similar. The differences lie in the genre (one being fiction and the other nonfiction) and the text features of each different style. By text features, we are referring to the format and purpose of a given text, including how the text is laid out on the page and how captions or headings are used to convey meaning, as when reading informational texts. What remains constant in both of these standards is the goal that students read complex texts and determine the key ideas and details using text-based evidence.

For guidance on helping your child with this standard, please refer to the following section in this chapter: How Can You Help Support Reading: Literature and Reading: Informational Text Standards?

Reading: Informational Text Standards

A huge change that Common Core ELA standards employs is separating the standards for teaching nonfiction or informational texts. As you might recall, the ELA standards call for a 50/50 split in grades K–5 in teaching fiction and informational text. Teaching informational text is quite different than teaching fiction. The text structures and themes of each require a different mental process. Teachers have to teach kids how to use pictures, graphs, and headings to determine key information in nonfiction text. They will also be exposed to texts at a higher grade-level band. Remember, those new Lexile levels have increased the complexity of the texts that your kids will be reading.

FACT

A key point about the Reading: Informational Text standards is that they focus on digital media as well as print. So in essence, "text" now relates to news clips, videos, and audio. This means that children will have to use their listening comprehension skills to build meaning from texts in varied media.

The Reading: Informational Text standards also focus on using informational texts to gain understandings that can be expressed to others. Students will be responsible for presenting information both orally and in written formats. Learning how to determine key information from informational texts is a very important skill. Teachers will need to help students acquire this skill because these text structures include a lot of information, and sifting through the texts to find relevant facts can be challenging.

How Can You Help Support Reading: Literature and Reading: Informational Text Standards?

One of the best ways to support the Reading: Literature and Reading: Informational Text standards at home is to encourage a love of reading in your child. When students love reading and spend time with books they become more proficient and excel in this area. The same is true with math.

ESSENTIAL

As a parent, the best way you can help support your child with the Reading: Informational Text standards is to provide him with nonfiction texts. The fact is, children love reading nonfiction and learning about the world they live in. Children are fascinated by nature, and how and why things work.

You can also support your child's learning by using multiple sources to explore a topic he is interested in. For example if your child is interested in farms, you could take your child on a field trip to a local farm, read a fictional story about farming, read informational texts about farming, and watch news clips about the subject. After each experience, have conversations with your child about what he learned. It will be interesting to hear what he comes up with. By having these multiple exposures to the subject of farming your child should be able to form opinions and elaborate on the subject.

Language Standards

The Language standards focus on grammar. Grammar is an often-overlooked component of instruction that many people shy away from. The authors of the Common Core provide a strong set of grammar standards that build in complexity across the grade levels. For instance, kindergarten students focus on nouns and verbs, and by 5th grade they master correct verb tense, prepositions, and conjunctions.

Proficient grammar skills are extremely valuable, and they build as each grade level progresses. Grammar is also important because it helps students in their writing, which is another very important literacy skill. The Language standards provide the criteria for effective grammar use, which is of significant importance when learning to read, write, and speak. The best way to support grammar at home is to remind your child to check his grammar when writing and to encourage your child to speak in complete sentences. We all have the tendency to slip into informal speech when we are at home. As often as possible model correct grammar so your child will have good models to follow.

Supporting the Language Standards

Teaching grammar can be fun and inventive if you look at it as a way to help your child become a better writer. One way to accomplish this is by having your child look at published writing. Discuss the language used and the use of punctuation in the text. Have your child try playing with text that he has written by using some of the grammar his favorite writers use. This can be especially effective when writing poetry. Poets are known for their clever use of punctuation. Again, use it as an exploratory process where your child is able to take risks in his grammar use as he explores new ways to use grammar.

Speaking and Listening Standards

The Common Core has specific standards for speaking and listening. These standards help students learn how to properly share oral information. These standards begin at a young age so that kids can develop these skills early, starting in kindergarten.

College students and workers alike are often called upon to present orally. For managers and company leaders, oral communication will be expected of them as they work with clients and coworkers. By building this confidence at an early age, students will be ready to speak and share information later in life.

ESSENTIAL

Glossophobia, or the fear of public speaking, is one of the top fears that people have. It is estimated that more than 70 percent of the population has some level of fear when asked to speak in public.

You can help support oral communication at home by having your child recite poetry aloud or have mini presentations to share information that she has learned at school. Another idea is to have your child participate in extracurricular activities that promote and require public speaking, including:

- Boy or Girl Scouts
- Key Club
- 4-H Club
- Junior Achievement
- Youth groups

These organizations are wonderful ways for students to build confidence and learn public speaking skills. Moreover, these organizations promote helping others, which is another important social skill.

Writing Standards

The Writing standards focus on the writing skills that are part of the Common Core. There are three main writing genres that the Common Core ELA standards focus on: arguments, explanatory, and narrative.

Students in all grade levels are expected to write arguments. How many of you have kids who like to question you? Well, the Writing standards are designed to help kids argue their points using information from texts that they read.

You can help your child with argumentative writing by asking him to write letters proposing why he wants to have a particular toy or attend a special event. Be sure to tell him that he has to tell you why you should consider his request. Make sure that your child gives details or evidence why his idea should be considered.

Explanatory writing is also referred to as informative writing. It focuses on giving facts, details, or examples. This would include writing about a report about a topic or writing directions on how to complete a task. Encourage this writing genre by having your child write a short report after attending an event or having your child write directions on how to play a game.

Finally, narrative writing includes writing fiction or nonfiction texts that tell a story. Children enjoy writing about their day at school or what they want to do on the weekend. You can encourage practice in this genre by having your child keep a journal where she can write for fun.

FACT

Many students find journal writing times one of their favorite times of the day. Today many schools have a time where kids are allowed to write in their journals. In some classrooms teachers have interactive journals where the child and the teacher correspond. You can do this at home by sharing a journal with your child where you write back and forth about your experiences.

What Can You Do At Home to Help with Writing?

To be a literate individual your child will need to have a strong base in writing. In order to become a good writer, your child must be a good reader. Writers read a lot and get ideas for their writing from what they read. They also learn about sentence structure and acquire vocabulary from reading. The skill and craft of writing is essential to literacy. Encourage your child to write, perhaps even suggesting that she keeps a journal. Even just a small spiral notebook to jot down thoughts and ideas is a way to encourage writing. You can also make digital writing tools available, including computer keyboards. To help your child become comfortable using a keyboard, allow her to type and practice writing on the computer. Your child can determine if she prefers writing by hand or via the computer. Many students like to create a handwritten draft of their work, and then use the computer for their final draft. You can work with your child to see which method works best for her.

CHAPTER 4

College and Career Anchor Standards for Reading

The central organizational structure of the Common Core ELA standards is housed under anchor standards. These anchor standards serve to differentiate the literacy goals of the ELA standards. The anchors are the more broad explanations of where students are headed as they progress through the grade levels. This chapter will define the anchor standards, discuss their importance, and look at ways they will impact your child's learning experience.

What Are Anchor Standards?

The overarching focus for the Common Core ELA standards is found in what are known as the "anchor standards." Anchor standards serve as an indicator of what the expectations are for students who are "college and career ready." These standards, formally called the College and Career Readiness anchor standards, go across all content areas from kindergarten through grade 12, and serve as a compass to show where the standards will ultimately take kids upon their graduation from high school. This is a novel concept because it gives both parents and teachers alike a full view of the intent of the intended standard. The structure of the anchors will be discussed in the next section. Anchor standards let us know what college readiness skills are required, and then to understand how we are to prepare our children to meet them. There are thirty-two anchor standards in ELA. They are organized as follows:

- 10 reading anchor standards (broken into Reading: Literature standards and Reading: Informational Texts standards)
- 10 writing anchor standards
- 6 speaking and listening anchor standards
- 6 language anchor standards

Teachers use these anchor standards to better understand what students need to be able to do by the end of their high school journey. These anchors guide the instruction along the way as our children are prepared for college and career. The anchor standards provide a clear picture of how the Common Core standards build upon one another as your child progresses from one grade level to the next. It is interesting to see how an anchor standard evolves from kindergarten all the way through high school.

The Common Core authors were very specific about the support and scaffolds that children need so that they may acquire skills as they progress through school. The following chapters will explore the thirty-two anchor standards in depth in an effort to provide you with an understanding of where the Common Core standards are taking students in grades K–5. Keep in mind that these anchors provide an indication of the necessary skills that students must have in order to exhibit college and career readiness upon high school graduation.

What Are the Key Ideas in Reading?

The reading anchors include ten anchor standards that are broken into four groups:

- Key Ideas and Details—three standards
- Craft and Structure—three standards
- Integration of Knowledge and Ideas—three standards
- Range and Level of Text Complexity—one standard

The reading anchor standards focus on providing students with the tools they need to be proficient, reflective readers. Some people refer to this as "reading like a detective," and this terminology actually has some merit to it. The standards require that students use evidence from the text to determine the key ideas and details of the text they read.

FACT

The primary goal of reading is comprehension. Requiring students to provide distinct evidence from the text supports this idea. Without comprehension of what is being read students are just reading words on a page without building any meaning.

Key Ideas and Details

There are three anchor standards under the Key Ideas and Details group. Reading anchor standard 1 says:

> Read closely to determine what the text says explicitly and to make logical inferences from it; cite specific textual evidence when writing or speaking to support conclusions drawn from the text.

Keep in mind that this anchor is where children are expected to be by the end of grade 12. There is a staircase of complexity that prepares children to meet each standard by the time they finish high school, meaning the standards become more involved as students move from one grade level to the next.

For children in grades K–5 anchor standard 1 revolves around the idea of closely reading texts to draw out the most important details and inferences that an author uses to convey a message. As you may have surmised, students will be expected to "read closely" to determine those key ideas and details. Close reading will be expected from them in their assignments, which will require that they cite the text in their responses to show where the ideas are coming from.

ESSENTIAL

Students will rarely be given tasks that require simple recall of facts. Most real-world reading tasks require the ability to read, acquire knowledge, and determine meaning.

What Is Close Reading?

Close reading is a buzzword in the field of education. As a learning method, its importance has risen since the inception of the Common Core ELA standards. In fact, the words "read closely" are the first words used in the anchor standard for reading. Educational scholars across the nation have worked diligently to develop close reading routines and lessons that teachers can use to teach children to closely read a text to find important facts and information.

FACT

As a parent, the most important thing to remember about close reading is that it is mindful reading. This type of reading requires your child to use the words and ideas from text to support any assumptions or conclusions he is drawing.

Close reading can be summed up as looking at a text and reading it intentionally to determine key ideas and themes. At home you'll want to model for your child the importance of reading and rereading a text to determine what the author's key points are. Long gone are the days of personal opinion. Students are now being required to support their conclusions with the texts being read. To better understand how close reading works in practical terms, consider the following process. First, ask your child to read this excerpt:

Fred and James were planning to visit their grandmother for the weekend. They were both excited to visit, but each had a reservation about spending so much time on the farm. Fred was going to miss out on a soccer game and James wanted to go fishing with his friends. They each knew their grandmother was really looking forward to their visit, so they each decided to sacrifice their own fun for a weekend with Grandma.

After reading the text ask your child the following question:
- Using evidence from the text give two examples of how James and Fred were feeling about the visit to Grandma's house.

This question is quite different from questions that may have been asked in the classroom in the past like, "Have you ever felt like James and Fred?" Or, "Would you rather visit your grandmother or spend time with friends?"

Note that the latter two questions do not require children to closely read the text in order to respond to the question. In fact, they could answer either question without ever reading the excerpt, and instead just rely on their background knowledge and personal ideas and opinions to arrive at an answer.

As this example illustrates, the Key Ideas and Details standard changes the way reading comprehension is taught and alters the expectations placed on students, because they must now justify their claims based on what they read.

Central Ideas

Under the Key Ideas and Details group, anchor standard 2 states:

Determine central ideas or themes of a text and analyze their development; summarize the key supporting details and ideas.

This standard builds upon the first anchor standard that requires the student to comprehend a text by close reading. This standard asks students to uncover the key focus of a text by examining how its details and ideas unfold.

ESSENTIAL

A good way to teach this concept of determining and analyzing the central idea of a text to your child is to think about the text as a tree. Once all the flowers, leaves, and fruits are taken away, what is left? Bare branches, of course. Similarly, the bare-bone details of a text are its central ideas. This standard is about getting to the heart of the matter. Just the facts and nothing more.

This standard prepares students to read large amounts of text, and then quickly and accurately determine key details and ideas. Consider high school and college textbooks: These texts are filled with dates, illustrations, maps, and figures. Students must be taught how to read this material so that they can determine what the most important and necessary information is on a particular subject.

This anchor standard highlights the importance of teaching kids to really look at text to determine key details and ideas. The ELA standards start teaching kids as early as kindergarten how to hone in on those key ideas and details.

FACT

Children need to communicate complex ideas in a succinct manner. People are very busy these days, and we live in an age where short news briefs are the norm. Being able to take large amounts of information and break it down into succinct and important details is a skill that will be increasingly important in the workforce.

An important term to remember is *summary*. Individuals who are college and career ready have the ability to summarize key information to determine the big ideas. You can support the learning of this concept with your child by asking him to summarize the key details in movies that you watch, books that you read, magazine articles, pamphlets, and so on. Helping your child learn to quickly and efficiently summarize key ideas by getting rid of the fluff is an essential skill to being college and career ready. As students move along the grade levels they will continue to build on this necessary skill base.

In grades K–5 this standard may be addressed by asking kids to write quick summaries on informational materials or by having a child write a tweet about something she has researched.

Character Analysis

The third Reading anchor standard under the umbrella of Key Ideas and Details looks at characters, characterization, plot, and setting. Standard 3 reads:

> Analyze how and why individuals, events, or ideas develop and interact over the course of a text.

At first glance this standard may seem similar to what has been done in classrooms for years, or it may appear to just be a repeat of the previous two standards. This standard differs because the aim is to help students study the development and interaction of characters, events, and ideas over the course of a text. It requires that students closely read the text in order to make these determinations.

A good example of this is the classic hero story. In these stories, a potentially heroic person starts out as a shell of herself. Possibly she is shy and unable to articulate her feelings at the start of the story, and by the end she evolves into a well-defined and stable character. A great story to use to teach kids this concept is the story of Ruby Bridges. It is an ideal read-aloud story for students who are in the 2nd and 3rd grade. Ruby Bridges was the little African American girl who was allowed entrance into a segregated school at the beginning of the civil rights movement. (You may recall Norman Rockwell's painting that depicted Ruby walking to school accompanied by federal marshals.) This story details the experience. Children can discuss the turning points of this story and the events that led to Ruby being triumphant in the end.

The goal is for students to understand how conflicts and interactions help mold our behaviors and character. This is a skill highly lauded in college and the workplace. In college, students will encounter texts about world figures and will have to analyze the actions that led to the person's rise or fall.

FACT

To help your child develop this skill of analyzing characters you can talk to him about the actions of characters in books and films, and then quiz your child on how those actions related to a particular character's final rise or fall.

The event that triggers the change in a character can be something positive, like someone providing a helping hand; or it can be negative, like the loss of a loved one. Many classic children's stories deal with these life-changing events that impact the lead character's destiny. (A good example of this can be found in the young adult novel *Holes* by Louis Sachar. In this novel students learn about the consequences of choices and how their choices can have a major impact on the future.)

Analytical thinking is an essential aspect of this third reading anchor standard. The integration of knowledge and ideas requires that students analyze events and characters to determine how they work together in the text and relate to the whole. Analysis skills are invaluable in the workplace because businesses are continually determining how actions and events reflect on current practice. Being good at this can allow an individual to predict general outcomes, which is something very important in the business world.

Craft and Structure

The craft and structure anchor standard also consists of three standards. These three standards focus on developing skills in word usage and text structures.

Word Choice

The fourth reading anchor standard focuses on the use of words. Reading anchor standard 4 reads:

Interpret words and phrases as they are used in a text, including determining technical, connotative, and figurative meanings, and analyze how specific word choices shape meaning and tone.

This anchor standard is about word choice. The standard asks students to determine three distinct aspects of word meaning: technical meaning, connotative or implied meaning, and figurative or nonliteral meaning. Let's take a minute to break down technical, connotative, and figurative meanings:

- **Technical Meaning:** Words that have a special or practical meaning in relation to the subjects being studied.

  Example: Photosynthesis is a technical term that explains the process used by plants to convert light energy.

- **Connotative Meaning:** Words or phrases that evoke feelings and emotions. The words will have concrete meanings, but the connotative meanings are the feelings the words evoke.

  Example: Holocaust. The concrete meaning of this word is great or complete devastation. However, the connotative meaning of this word goes far beyond a dictionary definition. It evokes pain and grief that children can understand by reading books about the Holocaust.

- **Figurative Meaning:** Words that have meanings behind the word choices. The meanings might be the opposite of what the authors wrote. For example, when using the term *bad* to describe something that is actually good.

  Example: That is one bad car.

College and career ready students are able to determine what a word means in relation to the text. For example, they will look at the types of words that an author uses to make the reader feel a mood (happy, sad, angry, glad, and so on). An author may, for example, describe a setting using only terms that convey distress so as to convey the state of mind of a character. An example would be a person looking at a rose garden and only seeing thorns instead of beautiful flowers.

This anchor is important because it teaches students to become succinct in their writing. This skill will come handy in the college setting. For instance, college students are required to write essays on different topics. There is usually a word-count limit that the professor imposes. Student success in this regard hinges on an ability to use only the most succinct and deliberate words to convey a message.

ESSENTIAL

This skill of choosing the right words is also important in public speaking and business writing. This anchor goes a long way in helping students learn to use words that convey precise and explicit meaning and tone. Being able to relay information in an abbreviated manner is increasingly important in the business world.

To help your child with this anchor standard try some of the following activities:

1. Have your child write a text using only a specific number of words. Remind him that the words he chooses must be deliberate to convey his intended message. You may have to provide context for the writing; for example, maybe a description of your child's room or a list of attributes that represent a good friend.
2. Read a poem with your child and discuss the words the poet uses. Ask your child how the words help to create the mood of the poem. You can use the works of Dr. Seuss or Shel Silverstein. Both of these authors have created poetry for children that is rich in language.
3. Listen to a new story and have your child write a news brief. Tell her to include only the most important fact that the listener will need. Remind your child of the importance of including the five W and one H questions (who, what, when, where, why, and how).

Text Structures

The fifth anchor standard in reading explores text structures. Anchor standard 5 reads:

Analyze the structure of texts, including how specific sentences, paragraphs, and larger portions of the text (e.g., a section, chapter, scene, or stanza) relate to each other and the whole.

In this standard, students are asked to closely analyze how parts of the text relate to the overall theme of the larger work. This involves closely analyzing scenes of stories and stanzas of poetry to clarify how they relate to the larger whole. For fictional texts this might mean creating feelings of suspense, and in informational texts conveying feelings of anger or sadness by using precise examples that promote these emotions. Reading anchor standard 6, the final anchor standard under the umbrella of craft and structure, reads:

> Assess how point of view or purpose shapes the content and style of a text.

This anchor, which relates to reading anchor standard 5, asks students to read a text and determine the author's purpose and point of view in writing the text. There is bias in writing. Often, underlying reasons determine the composition of a text. Students are expected to learn to read texts and determine the writer's intent. This can be accomplished by looking at the writing style, word choice, and organization of the text. This, again, requires that students closely read the text and look at the structure to draw these conclusions.

Integration of Knowledge and Ideas

Anchor standards 7, 8, and 9 fall under the Integration of Knowledge and Ideas, which is the next umbrella of the ELA anchor standards. These standards focus on the skill of closely analyzing a text to determine how illustrations and details in them relate to the key ideas. They also involve comparing texts to determine the key details. The most appropriate way to support this idea is to give your child an opportunity to study informational text features including graphs and charts to help gain meaning about the context of the information presented in the text. Students in grades K–5 will be taught about the importance of illustrations, charts, and graphs as they relate to comprehending texts.

Anchor standard 7 reads:

> Integrate and evaluate content presented in diverse media and formats, including visually and quantitatively, as well as in words.

The buzzword "wide reading" is often oversimplified. By suggesting wide reading, the Common Core authors are urging students to read multiple sources to gain knowledge. This idea supports reading texts, media, and other sources on a topic of interest.

This standard asks students to evaluate how the author's use of illustrations, graphs, multimedia, and so on affects the overall meaning of a text. This evaluation requires the ability to analyze the effects of different text features to convey meaning in fiction and nonfictional texts. You can help your child understand this concept by asking her to look at the charts in a text and discuss how the author's use of the chart will help the reader understand the concept. If there is more than one chart, you could ask your child to share which chart provides the better visual representation to help the reader. Finally, ask your child to provide any examples of changes she would make to the chart to help the reader understand the concept.

Anchor standard 8 reads:

Delineate and evaluate the argument and specific claims in a text, including the validity of the reasoning as well as the relevance and sufficiency of evidence.

The key idea of this anchor is to determine if the claims in an argument are valid. This involves understanding valid reasoning and the use of valid resources. Students may struggle with this, as many tend to think that everything written is true. Identifying and avoiding bias in writing is an important skill for the college and career ready student. The standards under this anchor will help students begin to critically evaluate what they read. Help your child understand that not everything that is written is true and often authors are biased and bring in their personal opinions when shaping an argument. You can practice this skill by looking at television commercials, which often have a spin to make the audience believe the product is better than others or will make an individual stronger or more popular by using them. Commercials for sports drinks or athletic footwear are classic at building these arguments.

Anchor standard 9, the final anchor standard under the umbrella of integration of knowledge and ideas, reads:

Analyze how two or more texts address similar themes or topics in order to build knowledge or to compare the approaches the authors take.

This standard encourages students to read multiple texts on a subject in order to analyze themes and author approach. The ability to compare and contrast is imperative to students in the workforce and college. This standard encourages reading multiple sources, which in turn will build a student's knowledge of a topic, which will increase the child's knowledge base and ability to analyze a topic. The more students read on a subject the more knowledgeable they will become. Encouraging your child to read fiction, nonfiction, and any other sources that relate to a subject that he has a strong interest in is a great way to support this standard. When I was in college I found that my classmates who read all the supplemental extra articles and books had a lot more to say during class discussions. This holds true for your child. If your child is learning about volcanoes, take a trip to the library and search online for as many resources that you can find on the subject. Explore the topic with your child and discuss the information that is presented in the different texts. Discuss what is similar and what points are different.

Range and Level of Text Complexity

The final category of the ELA anchors in reading is Range and Level of Text Complexity. As noted in Chapter 2, the Common Core ELA shift 2 presents students with an increase in text complexity. This anchor standard focuses on the ability of students to read and comprehend complex texts. Anchor standard 10 reads:

Read and comprehend complex literary and informational texts independently and proficiently.

The key idea to remember in regard to this anchor standard is that students will be reading texts with increasingly high Lexile levels, and will do so with independence and proficiency. To accomplish this task, students will be asked to struggle with complex texts in an effort to build their stamina and confidence in reading such texts. This standard calls for teaching kids to persevere and read such texts with confidence. The best way to encourage perseverance in reading texts is to teach your child to pace herself when she has a large amount to read. Often children become discouraged when they have a large text to read. Teaching your child to break the task up into manageable chunks is a great strategy to employ. Teach your child to read the text in smaller chunks such as one paragraph at a time, and then to write notes about what she has read. The more she practices this skill, the more text she will be able to read in one setting without having to stop.

CHAPTER 5

College and Career Anchor Standards for Writing

The ability to communicate effectively and efficiently in different written formats is an important skill for college and career ready individuals. In college, students will be required to write on different subject matters in both the humanities and technical areas. Writing can also be an important aspect in the workforce. Writing e-mails, memos, and notes is an everyday activity in many fields of work. These ten writing anchor standards help prepare students to write confidently in diverse content areas and for diverse purposes. This chapter focuses on the writing anchor standards and the changes they support in the teaching of writing in the classroom.

What Are the Key Ideas in Writing?

The writing anchors include ten anchor standards that are broken into four groups:

- Text Types and Purposes—three standards
- Production and Distribution of Writing—three standards
- Research to Build and Present Knowledge—three standards
- Range of Writing—one standard

The Common Core writing anchor standards focus on supporting ideas using evidence from text. Just as this instructional shift was evident in the examination of the reading anchors, so this shift is evident in the writing anchors. Students are called to explain their ideas using text-based evidence. As in the reading standards, opinions must be backed up with textual evidence, and personal opinions are not relevant.

FACT

Remember that anchor standards indicate where children are expected to be by the end of grade 12. The grade-level standards provide a staircase of complexity that prepares children to meet each anchor standard by the time they finish high school.

For years students were given writing prompts as a catalyst for their writing. These prompts focused on things like, "Write a letter to your school principal stating why you support summer vacation," or "Write about a day you spent at the park with a friend." It is now commonplace for students to read a text or multiple texts and digital sources and respond to its content in writing. Keep in mind that the texts that students are reading in the Common Core are more rigorous and have more complex themes. With these changes, responding in writing will require analytical thinking and analysis. This means that students will have to go back into the text and use words and examples from the text in their written responses.

Another change to acknowledge is that text refers to not only written text but also videos and other multimedia sources. Students will be asked to respond in writing to news clips and media streams—again, something very different from what we have seen in the past. Students will need to think of media as a form of communication and learn to extract the most important details from this medium to incorporate into their writing pieces.

ESSENTIAL

More and more people are using digital sources to get news. In fact, in recent years subscriptions to paper newspapers and magazines have declined because consumers are increasingly reading news online and opting for digital versions of magazines. This shift prompts the importance of teaching children to interact with these media sources, extrapolate information, and write.

The writing standards focus on three main types of writing:

- Persuasive/opinion and argument
- Informational/functional
- Narrative

For each writing type the standards' complexities build from year to year. For example, argumentative writing in kindergarten is done with support from the teacher. As students progress through the grades, this scaffolding and support gradually fades away as students develop these skills.

Text Types and Purposes

The first three writing anchor standards fall under the umbrella of Text Types and Purposes.

Writing Arguments and Opinions

Writing anchor standard 1 asks student to write arguments. This standard reads:

Write arguments to support claims in an analysis of substantive topics of texts using valid reasoning and relevant and sufficient evidence.

This standard focuses on supporting arguments in writing by using text-based evidence. When referring to the term *argument*, the standard calls for the performance of and ability to back up research with substantive evidence. In college, students will be required to write research papers and support their claims with relevant evidence from the research conducted. This skill begins in kindergarten as teachers model the importance of using text-based evidence when presenting arguments. Students have to understand how to get information on a topic from sources and pull out the most relevant information from each to include in a paper.

Arguments and opinion pieces are an important type of writing that students must master. Anchor standard 1 requires that students provide sufficient supporting reasons to clarify their stand on an issue. This requirement is different from past standards, which allowed students to back up their opinions with little to no support that was based on what the student had read or seen. Previously students could write essays or respond to writing tasks without providing evidence from the text. This was also the case in reading. The Common Core now asks students to refer to the text in their responses as a way to support their findings.

FACT

A way to support this writing anchor standard on arguments/opinion pieces at home is to have your child write about her opinion on any topic. Require that she give at least two supporting reasons based on the text or media source. This is great practice for the type of writing that will be required in college and in the workplace.

Informative and Explanatory Writing

The second writing anchor standard that falls under the category of Text Types and Purposes builds on the skill of responding to informative/explanatory texts. Writing anchor standard 2 reads:

Write informative/explanatory texts to examine and convey complex ideas and information clearly and accurately through the effective selection, organization, and analysis of content.

The key word to remember about this standard is *analysis*. This writing anchor standard calls for analysis of informational and technical texts. The following is a list of sources where you might find informative and explanatory texts:

INFORMATIVE TEXTS/EXPLANATORY TEXTS
- Newspapers
- Brochures
- Websites
- Magazines
- Maps
- Textbooks
- Videos (documentaries)
- Manuals
- Encyclopedias
- Menus
- Travel guides
- Advertisements
- Commercials

The ability to read information, organize ideas, select key points, and then analyze the text is the goal to fulfilling the standard when writing in response to informative/explanatory texts. Some of the key skills that this anchor standard calls for are clarity and accuracy. The first step for accomplishing these skills is to understand the different informative/explanatory text types in order to determine which ideas are most significant. Students in grades K–5 will continually work on selecting key points and organizing them in order to respond to writing tasks. They will work on these skills in both reading and writing.

FACT

The reading and writing standards are parallel. For years schools have separated the instruction of reading and writing. In college courses the subjects are taught simultaneously in the English classroom. Schools are taking a cue from this and beginning to see how important it is to teach both subjects together.

This anchor standard is also specific in requiring that students write informative/explanatory texts by effectively selecting, organizing, and analyzing the content. This standard has a lot of components that students have to grasp in order to be college ready. They must first select appropriate information to include in their writing, and then effectively organize the writing to convey meaning. The best way to learn how to organize explanatory/informative writing is to read and study the components of nonfiction text.

ESSENTIAL

Parents can support this informative and explanatory standard by calling their children's attention to different text types. Look at a DVD manual or a report and talk about the structure of the text. Bring attention to the headers used, the language choice, and the information shared.

The final component of this writing standard calls for analyzing content. Analyzing is a skill that the Common Core ELA standards hit on continually. College and career ready individuals can effectively analyze information for comprehension and communication. In grades K–5 students will continually analyze content in reading and writing when they determine which information is reliable and most appropriate. These skills require students to analyze information critically so they can make informed decisions.

ALERT

Critical analysis skills are imperative in the workplace. Each day decisions are made that require careful analysis of outcomes. Being able to quickly and efficiently make judgments is a pertinent skill.

Narrative Writing

The third standard that falls under the category of Text Types and Purposes focuses on narrative writing. Narrative writing is typically a style of writing that children enjoy and are very comfortable with. This style of writing is entertaining, and children typically connect to it.

Writing anchor standard 3 reads:

Write narratives to develop real or imagined experiences of events using effective techniques, well-chosen details, and well-structured event sequences.

Narrative writing requires an ability to communicate stories in an organized and effective way. Storytelling is important because people typically connect to stories.

This standard asks students to write well-developed stories with well-chosen details and well-structured event sequences. In grades K–5 these elements refer to plot, the use of dialogue, and using effective details.

ALERT

Recent studies have shown that writing skills of U.S. students have declined. Despite our technological advances (spell check, online dictionaries) students struggle to communicate in written forms.

There are specific features that are associated with the different narrative types. Each is listed below.

NARRATIVE STORY WRITING SHOULD INCLUDE:
- Characters and setting
- A sense of story: beginning, middle, and end
- Ending with a resolution or outcome

BIOGRAPHICAL WRITING SHOULD INCLUDE:
- Information about date and place of birth
- Information about family and early life
- Major life events
- Key contributions

NARRATIVE POETRY WRITING SHOULD:
- Include a character and plot
- Move beyond lyrical poems

Examples of narrative poetry include "Casey at the Bat," "The Raven," and "The Rime of the Ancient Mariner."

The Common Core standards require that narrative writing be focused. The writing should include only the most relevant information needed to convey meaning. Dialogue should be used to enhance meaning, and pacing should be appropriate to ensure reader interest. These skills are enhanced by reading classic literature and discussing story elements.

Teaching text structures is a great way to allow children to understand the purpose for writing in different genres. It is also a great way to help children monitor their comprehension.

Production and Distribution of Writing

There are three standards that fall under the category of Production and Distribution of Writing. These standards focus on producing writing that is clear and directed. They call for coherence in writing and a focus on audience. All writing is communicative in nature and has an intended audience, and the three Production and Distribution of Writing standards clarify these writing skills.

The Writing Task

Writing anchor standard 4 reads:

Produce clear and coherent writing in which the development, organization, and style are appropriate to task, purpose, and audience.

The first area of focus in this anchor standard is attending to the writing task. This can be writing an essay, memo, report, or other type of writing. The student must become skilled in determining the appropriate style to use, which in turn will produce the tone of the writing.

This standard also focuses on ensuring that the writer considers the intended audience. This consideration determines the tone and vocabulary used in the writing piece. For instance, when writing a letter to a friend you would use different language than when writing a letter to a school principal.

Finally, this standard focuses on determining the purpose of the written piece. The purpose might be to entertain, persuade, inform, and so forth. This standard is designed to help students understand the task, purpose, and audience when constructing written pieces.

FACT

Many teachers use mentor texts to provide models of how to write. Mentor texts are pieces of writing used to model any aspect of the writing craft. For instance, teachers use *The Wonderful Wizard of Oz* to teach about characterization. Students can discuss how the lead characters interact and help to build their stories through their interaction. They will use this knowledge to build characters that are more believable and life-like.

Having your child write thank you notes, menus, and letters is a great way to practice this writing anchor standard. Being comfortable writing in different styles is a quality shared by college and career ready individuals.

Following is a pre-writing process you can use with your child. It will help your child determine what he will write about, who he will write it for, and how he will communicate the message.

TOPIC
- What is the focus for the writing?
- What are you writing about?

AUDIENCE
- Who is going to read this text?
- Who is your target audience?

PURPOSE
- Why am I writing this?
  - To inform
  - To persuade
  - To explain
  - To entertain
  - To instruct

Revising and Editing

The second standard under the category of Production and Distribution of Writing is writing anchor standard 5. Standard 5 reads:

Develop and strengthen writing as needed by planning, revising, editing, rewriting, or trying a new approach.

This writing anchor standard focuses on the need for students to revise and edit their writing pieces so as to strengthen them. The revision and editing process is important in both college and the workplace. In college it is important because students are graded on their ability to write pieces with minimal grammatical and content errors. This is only possible by going through the editing and revision process.

FACT

In the workplace, editing is important. Skilled writers dedicate time in their work schedule to review e-mail communications and memos. These professionals understand that there is nothing worse than sending out an e-mail without first reviewing it to fix grammatical and content errors.

Teachers will begin to build on the level of skill in the editing cycle during classroom instruction. This instruction might include having a writing schedule that allows for editing. Teachers can also help students recognize the importance of editing because doing so will help them achieve better grades and produce writing that is of higher quality. Instilling this important step of editing and revising in the writing process is an important skill to highlight. Encourage your child to re-read his writing pieces to ensure they have clarity. The revision process can be intimidating at first. Make the revision process stress-free by reminding your child it is part of the writing cycle.

The final section of the standard mentions rewriting or trying a new approach. This can be a tricky idea to get across to students. They often have a particular writing style that they feel comfortable with and therefore see no need to try a new approach. A way to bridge this issue is for students to read the papers of other writers. Students in Common Core–supported classrooms will do this routinely by way of peer editing during the revision process. Indeed, this is a great way to help students try new writing approaches.

Publishing and Collaboration

The final standard that falls under Production and Distribution of Writing is writing anchor standard 6. This standard reads:

Use technology, including the Internet, to produce and publish writing and to interact and collaborate with others.

Using digital tools to produce writing is another shift for the Common Core ELA standards. This writing anchor standard supports digitally publishing pieces of writing. To prepare students to be successful in this particular digital-age period and beyond, it is necessary that teachers require them to use technology to produce writing. Skilled use of digital technology is now the norm in colleges and most high schools. It is now also prominent in many elementary schools. Having your child use technology to produce writing is a good practice.

This anchor standard also notes the idea of collaboration using digital tools. Students can work in teams as they edit their writing using real-time platforms like Google Docs (*www.google.com/docs/about*). New and evolving technology options like these allow students the ability to receive feedback on their writing from their peers as they work.

FACT

Most American classrooms have technology including computer labs and one-to-one devices for student use. Encourage practice and skill building on these devices in preparation for your child's college research and future career skills.

Collaboration is a skill that will be helpful to students after graduation from high school when they work on team documents in college and the workplace. Group writing assignments are often used in college courses. Preparing kids for this experience in elementary school is an important step. Collaboration is a necessary work skill. Having your child work with others is something you can encourage by getting her involved in sports and other team activities. Working in isolation is not typically the norm in today's world.

Research to Build and Present Knowledge

Three writing anchor standards fall under this category. The standards focus on conducting research and gathering information.

Sustained Research

The first anchor standard under this category is writing anchor standard 7, which reads:

Conduct short as well as more sustained research projects based on focused questions, demonstrating understanding of the subject under investigation.

Research writing is important in the Common Core standards. Students must be comfortable conducting investigations so that they can write quality research pieces. This research can be exhaustive when writing a formal research paper or it can be short when participating in an in-class writing assignment. Students need to be comfortable completing both tasks.

Teachers begin to instruct students about research writing in kindergarten. With teacher support, students begin writing short research reports in the early primary grades. This writing anchor standard provides a scaffold for instruction in research writing so that students come to college ready to conquer it. Research can come in the form of finding a good ballpark to visit or the finding best pizza in town. Having your child help to research these venues is a nice way to expose her to the research process in a non-threatening manner.

Proper Use and Citation of Source Materials

The next standard under Research to Build and Present Knowledge is writing anchor standard 8. This standard reads:

Gather relevant information from multiple print and digital sources, assess the credibility and accuracy of each source, and integrate the information while avoiding plagiarism.

Every college ready student must know how to properly cite references so as to avoid plagiarism. Plagiarism is when you present the work of someone else as your own. Many times students are not intentionally plagiarizing, in that they are not copying someone else's paper as their own, but they may use information from a text and not cite it in the body of the paper. Students will be introduced to proper citation so that they may avoid this pitfall.

ESSENTIAL

Plagiarism is a big problem for many college students. Most students plagiarize unknowingly because they are not aware of how to cite their references. Beginning to talk to students about proper citation is an important skill base to begin in elementary school.

Another key idea in this anchor standard is finding relevant sources. We live in an age of information. Some of the information online is good and some is not. Students will need to learn how to sift through information in an effort to determine the relevancy and validity of what they find. This can only be accomplished by understanding what differentiates valid sources from invalid sources. This will require that they read the texts carefully to find false information, and discover which sources do not use current research. Having these skills is important for success in both college and the workplace. Encourage this skill set by talking about the different resources available on a given topic. Talk about who wrote the information and if they provide information that is substantiated or based on evidence.

Using Evidence to Support Analysis

The final standard under the category of Research to Build and Present Knowledge is writing anchor standard 9. This standard reads:

Draw evidence from literary or informational texts to support analysis, reflection, and research.

The ability to analyze the resources used in a text is an important skill. Students will be taught to use only the most relevant pieces of information that help to establish the purpose of the writing. This will require a careful analysis of the resource and only including quotes and information that help establish the goal of writing the piece. This is a necessary step so kids can prove they are drawing evidence from the text. Again, expressing the importance of looking at the evidence in the text and only using the most pertinent information is important. By discussing text and determining which facts are more relevant you can support your child in building this skill.

ESSENTIAL

Common citation styles used in college are the American Psychological Association (APA) and the Modern Language Association (MLA). For more information on both styles check out the following websites: *www.mla.org; www.apastyle.org.*

Range of Writing

The final category for the writing anchor standards calls for a range of writing. There is one standard that falls under this category. Writing anchor standard 10 reads:

Write routinely over extended time frames (a long enough period of time that allows for research, reflection, and revision) and shorter time frames (a single sitting or over a day or two) for a range of tasks, purposes, and audiences.

Extended Writing

This standard matches the same idea as the reading anchor standard 10. It requires students to employ perseverance to write over extended time periods. It can be challenging for students to stick with a piece of writing for an extended period of time. Many students just want to write the paper and be done with it.

This writing standard requires students to write, put the work aside, reflect, and then write again. This is an important skill for students to develop. Doing so, however, requires time management skills. If a student waits until the last minute to write his essay, there will be no time for this necessary reflection.

This skill will be modeled in the classroom through a teaching method that requires an extensive editing and revision cycle for the creation of written work.

Short Time Frames

The standard also calls for students to write in short time frames, including a single sitting. This means students should be comfortable when responding to quick writing assignments in the classroom. Teachers will incorporate timed writing activities to help students build their stamina in writing extended responses in single sittings.

All of the writing anchor standards focus on providing students with the tools they need to produce writing that is clear, concise, and relevant. This too is an important skill that the college and career ready individual should possess.

CHAPTER 6

College and Career Anchor Standards for Speaking and Listening

This chapter covers the standards that address the ability to speak in different contexts and situations with different audiences. Doing so with confidence is an important skill that students should have before they enter into college and the workplace. College and career ready students have the ability to do more than read and write effectively; they also can speak in front of an audience with confidence and clarity. The authors of the Common Core included specific standards that address speaking and its reciprocal, listening. This chapter will focus on the six speaking and listening anchor standards, provide information about the skills associated with these standards, and offer relevant examples of how to support these standards at home.

What Are the Key Ideas in Speaking and Listening?

No other skill is as important as the ability to effectively communicate. Throughout history the oration skills of public speakers, like John F. Kennedy, Dr. Martin Luther King Jr., and Winston Churchill, have impressed and swayed people.

People associate intelligence and learnedness with the ability to articulate thoughts and ideas orally. In college, students will be called on to present information both as individuals and in group settings. In the workplace, oral presentations come in the form of keynote speeches, group trainings, and department meetings. In all of these contexts speaking clearly to articulate vision, mission, and goals is imperative. The ability to speak in public is a crucial skill for the college and career ready individual.

The speaking and listening anchor standards focus on the skills necessary for students to learn in primary and high school so that they can communicate orally in the college and work setting. Teachers, through the use of the standards, will help students to listen effectively, communicate with diverse individuals in group settings, express ideas in a clear and concise manner, and present information logically so that others can follow the train of thought of an argument.

The speaking and listening anchors consist of six standards. These standards are broken into two categories. The first category is Comprehension and Collaboration. As the category titles denote, comprehension and collaboration is the overarching umbrella for Speaking and Listening standards 1–3. The second category is Presentation of Knowledge and Ideas. Speaking and Listening standards 4–6 fall under this category, and they focus on oral presentation.

Comprehension and Collaboration

The three anchor standards in the category of comprehension and collaboration are designed to help students communicate effectively in a group setting, integrate and evaluate information, and assess a speaker's point of view. All of these skills work together to ensure students express themselves orally in a manner that is clear and easy to follow for an audience.

Effective Group Communication

The first anchor standard that falls under the category of comprehension and collaboration covers effective group communication. The standard reads:

> Prepare for and participate effectively in a range of conversations and collaborations with diverse partners, building on others' ideas and expressing their own clearly and persuasively.

This standard emphasizes the skill of listening to others' ideas in order to gain clarity, working with different partners and groups, and expressing one's own ideas clearly. This is a very sophisticated skill to possess. High school students who leave the 12th grade with mastery of this skill will be ready to succeed in college and the workplace. Let's break this anchor down into its key components.

Range of Conversations

This standard helps students engage in a range of conversations and collaborations. Upon leaving high school, students should be able to participate effectively in group conversations and collaborations. This standard promotes the idea of students working in diversified groups as they prepare for projects and collaborative assignments.

This standard calls for students to develop the skill of active listening so that they can effectively participate in group-based projects. This standard emphasizes the social skills of collaboration and active listening that help students make effective contributions to group efforts. Having your child be involved in social activities that encourage collaboration is a great way to help support this anchor standard outside of the classroom.

Diverse Partners

Working with diverse partners is another skill the standard emphasizes. Keep in mind the fact that these standards are preparing students for college and career. Let's turn to the workplace for a minute. As we become a more global society students will have to interact with people from other nations more and more in the workplace. Being able to work well with others of different diversities is an important skill to possess.

Building on Ideas of Others

This anchor standard also requires that students build on the ideas of others by expressing their own ideas in a clear and persuasive manner. This involves actively listening to what the other person is saying and then formulating a response that is original and builds on the topic. Students do not merely repeat what the other person says but acknowledge that other person's ideas and then express their own take on the topic at hand.

ESSENTIAL

Researchers have found a connection between listening comprehension and academic achievement. Active listening is an important skill to instill in your child.

This is not something that can be taught overnight. This skill involves listening, comprehending the other person's viewpoint, formulating an opinion based on the other person's point, and then expressing the idea orally. This involves understanding how to ask clarifying questions that help increase understanding and decrease misconceptions. Communication is a two-way street that involves listening, clarifying, and evaluating. If any of these steps are skipped, miscommunication can result.

Helping Students Master This Anchor Standard

This is one of those critical anchor standards that needs to be modeled by the teacher explicitly so that students can understand the thought processes involved. Encourage your child to listen carefully so she can ask clarifying questions. Often students need help attending to the speaker. Encourage your child to attend to the information being presented by leaning in and really listening with the purpose of understanding. She can then formulate questions to clarify meaning.

Integrating and Evaluating Information

The second standard that falls under the category of Comprehension and Collaboration involves the skill of integrating and evaluating information. The standard reads:

Integrate and evaluate information presented in diverse media and formats, including visually, quantitatively, and orally.

The skills of integration and evaluation are emphasized in this anchor standard. Students must learn how to pull together and integrate information that is gathered from multiple sources. This can mean using information from a journal article, textbook, podcast, video clip, and so forth. The skills necessary to complete this task include an understanding of how to include only the most relevant information from each source and leave out all the fluff.

ALERT

Elementary-age children often struggle with bringing in resources from multiple sources and maintaining comprehension. Note-taking skills are a good way to help children keep a hold on important information.

As already noted, the texts that students will be reading are more complex and will contain sophisticated ideas and themes. This means that students will have a lot of information to sift through. Students will need to hold on to the information from the different sources, and effectively integrate them into one cohesive form. Doing so involves teaching kids note-taking skills such that they can effectively manage important information from different sources. Graphic organizers are great too to use for note taking. One introductory graphic organizer that can be used for students in grades K–5 is the KWL chart. The KWL chart is a graphic organizer used in any context to help students learn about a topic. KWL is an acronym for What I **k**now, What I **w**ant to know, and What I **l**earned. Here is a sample KWL chart to use with your child.

K	W	L
*What I **K**now*	*What I **W**ant to Know*	*What I **L**earned*

Point of View

The third anchor standard under the Speaking and Listening anchor treats the concept of point of view. The standard reads:

Evaluate a speaker's point of view, reasoning, and use of evidence and rhetoric.

By the end of high school, students are expected to evaluate the purpose behind an author's point of view. This involves determining who the author is and who the intended audience is.

ESSENTIAL

Although this anchor standard is related to using these skills when speaking, the Common Core ELA standards are interchangeable between reading, writing, and speaking. In other words, these same skills and concepts are expected of students in the areas of reading and writing, in addition to speaking.

Marketing teams are experts at using reasoning and evidence to accomplish their desired goal—selling their product. Words are carefully chosen to convey the intended image and emotional feeling that the writer wants to evoke in the listener. To better understand the intended purpose, think about car commercials. They often conjure feelings of exhilaration and fun when driving in that shiny new sports car. If selling a family van, marketers instead convey meanings of safety and lots of room for the family. Marketers use words that convey the impression of safety, family, and comfort to convince particular consumers to purchase that new minivan. These are simplistic examples of point of view and focus that can assist students in developing an understanding of the concept. Clarifying the author's point of view will help your child comprehend text. Helping your child identify the author's purpose in writing will help him determine the point of view. Ask your child if the author wrote the piece to entertain, inform, or persuade. By determining the author's purpose in writing, your child can then determine the point of view.

FACT

Most people use the same vocabulary words continually. Making a concerted effort is necessary to build a more robust vocabulary. Introduce new words to your child on a regular basis, and encourage creativity when describing things or initiating discussions.

Presentation of Knowledge and Ideas

There are three standards that fall under this category. These anchor standards focus on preparing students to speak in different forums with confidence and clarity.

Presenting Information

The first anchor standard under presentation of knowledge and ideas is anchor standard 4, which reads:

Present information, findings, and supporting evidence such that listeners can follow the line of reasoning and the organization, development, and style are appropriate to task, purpose, and audience.

The ability to communicate orally so that the listener can follow the speaker's line of reasoning requires students to prepare their speeches in a succinct manner. You can encourage this skill by having your child practice her speech aloud before presenting at school. You can provide feedback to help her tweak her speech to ensure clarity.

Using Media

The second anchor standard under presentation of knowledge and ideas is anchor standard 5. Standard 5 reads:

Make strategic use of digital media and visual displays of data to express information and enhance understanding of presentations.

Using digital media sources and digital displays is a great way to provide supporting evidence for presentations. Knowing the best digital source to include requires prior preparation and understanding of who your audience is. Having conversations with your child about the intended audience and purpose for his presentation will enable him to choose the most appropriate supporting digital and visual displays.

Demonstrating Mastery

The final anchor standard listed under presentation of knowledge and ideas is anchor standard 6. Standard 6 reads:

Adapt speech to a variety of contexts and communicative tasks, demonstrating command of formal English when indicated or appropriate.

The ability to communicate orally using appropriate language indicates the need to teach students to use proper grammar and word usage when presenting formal presentations. Students can learn from models by watching newscasts or other presentations. As you watch the presentations, talk about the word choice used by the speaker. As your child continues to see these models she will start to incorporate them into her own presentations.

CHAPTER 7

College and Career Anchor Standards for Language

The final set of anchor standards for English language arts focuses on language. In the Common Core these language anchor standards focus on grammar and vocabulary. These language anchors clarify the skills students need to have in order to be proficient in using standard English in both the written and spoken formats. Proper grammar and vocabulary usage are important skills to possess. Being able to write confidently using the right words is important in the business world and in college. This chapter will focus on the language anchor standards and their implications for classroom instruction.

What Are the Key Ideas in Language?

The ability to use precise vocabulary when speaking and writing, and having a firm grasp on punctuation, are skills that college and career ready individuals possess. People are judged greatly by their written communication and vocabularies. In fact, a recent study showed that people with good vocabularies get better jobs and better pay.

The Common Core authors included six standards that fall under the umbrella of language. There are three categories listed for the language anchor standards. Those categories are:

- Category 1: Conventions of Standard English
- Category 2: Knowledge of Language
- Category 3: Vocabulary Acquisition and Use

There are two anchor standards listed under Category 1: Conventions of Standard English. One standard is listed under Category 2: Knowledge of Language. And three standards are listed under Category 3: Vocabulary Acquisition and Use.

FACT

College students are continually called upon to write. Having a firm grasp on the mechanics of English and a robust vocabulary will ensure that students are able to effectively communicate. In the workplace these same skills will ensure that communication is clear and concise.

Conventions of Standard English

The English language anchor standards are the most cut and dry of the standards. These anchors focus on the skills necessary to write, speak, and use academic vocabulary to convey meaning. These skills are necessary to be successful in the workplace and in college.

Language Standard 1

The first anchor standard that falls under the category of Conventions of Standard English is Language standard 1. The standard reads:

Demonstrate command of the conventions of standard English grammar and usage when writing or speaking.

This anchor standard proposes that college and career ready students have a command of the conventions of English grammar and usage, and apply them when speaking and writing. You may wonder what the authors mean by "command of the conventions." This refers to the ability to spell correctly and use appropriate grammar and conventions. Some of the skills this anchor refers to include the proper use of verbs, nouns, and pronouns. This anchor also refers to using punctuation correctly and choosing proper vocabulary to convey meaning. All of these are skills that students should master and be able to effortlessly execute upon high school graduation. By the end of 5th grade, students should have a firm grasp on standard English conventions and grammar usage. These standards build from one grade level to the next.

Language Standard 2

The second anchor standard under the language anchors is Language Standard 2. The standard reads:

Demonstrate command of the conventions of standard English capitalization, punctuation, and spelling when writing.

This anchor focuses on three very important aspects of grammar not included in the previous standard: capitalization, punctuation, and spelling. These primary and basic grammar skills hold great importance in today's world. Many young people like texting and tweeting, which are forms of communication that don't call for close attention to spelling and grammar. That is why this anchor is so important. There is nothing more embarrassing than turning in a work memo with spelling and grammar errors, or turning in a college paper with the same.

Seventy-five percent of English spellings are regular, and 400 or so are irregularly spelled words that are commonly used.

As a parent, you can model proper grammar and spelling usage with your child. Following are some games you can play to emphasize grammar and spelling.

Grammar

ACTIVITY TITLE: PUNCTUATION SEARCH

- Have your child circle different punctuation in the newspaper. You can highlight question marks, periods, and so forth. Depending on your child's age and grade level you can ask him to identify more complex punctuation.

ACTIVITY TITLE: SELF-EDITING

- Have your child edit a piece of writing. Write a paragraph and purposely make grammatical mistakes. Then allow your child to find the errors. This is a great way to emphasize the importance of editing.

Spelling

ACTIVITY TITLE: SPELLING FUN

- Using magnetic letters, have your child practice spelling words from class. If your child's teacher does not send home a spelling list, ask for a list of the high-frequency words that your child is responsible for and have your child practice spelling them.

ACTIVITY TITLE: RAINBOW SPELLING

- Give your child different colored pencils, crayons, or markers and have him practice spelling words in a rainbow of colors. Your child can do this by writing the words in one color and then writing on top of them with another color to create rainbow-spelled words.

Knowledge of Language

There is only one anchor standard under this category. That standard is Language Standard 3. The standard reads:

> Apply knowledge of language to understand how language functions in different contexts, to make effective choices for meaning or style, and to comprehend more fully when reading or listening.

This standard is about using proper word choice to convey meaning when communicating. Choosing the right words to convey the intended meaning when reading and writing is essential for communication. For instance, this standard supports teaching the skill of effective word usage. Skilled poets and writers are proficient in this skill set. They know just the perfect words to use to convey meaning. Think of Shakespeare and Emily Dickinson. Each used carefully chosen words to evoke meaning and feelings.

Teaching this language skill involves reading a variety of texts and examining the vocabulary and word choices used by the authors. This is the best way to show students how authors use words to express meaning in different contexts.

ALERT

Using precise words to express meaning can be accomplished by using idioms.

When applying this anchor standard, both fiction and nonfiction texts are used. Word choice is just as important in nonfiction as it is in fiction. Think about the language used in news stories and documentaries. These authors also use words to create meaning and evoke feelings in the listener. For example, think about the commercials for the ASPCA or Feed The Nation. The carefully written scripts of these commercials use language to evoke feelings in the audience so that the audience might contribute to a cause. Students will spend a lot of time looking at an author's word choice and determining how those choices affect the mood and tone of the text.

Vocabulary

There is a lot to be said about the importance of vocabulary instruction.

ALERT

By the time a child enters kindergarten she should have 4,000–5,000 words in her vocabulary.

In recent times we have been seeing more students on average entering kindergarten who know far fewer words. This deficiency is known as a word gap. Students who enter kindergarten with limited vocabulary struggle with comprehension. A word gap is difficult to bridge. For many children it continues throughout the early schooling years, and by the time these students enter 5th grade their comprehension is limited, which in turn affects their ability to read to learn.

Word Choice

The language anchor standard reiterates the importance of vocabulary so that students may use words with precision. This word choice skill is expanded upon as students move through the grade bands. Please note that this standard begins in grade 2 (students are building vocabulary knowledge in grades K–1).

The easiest way to support this standard at home is to talk about vocabulary and word choice when you are reading with your child. Consider using the following template to help lead the conversations:

Word	Meaning
What do you think this word means?	What does the word _____ mean in this text?
Why do you think the author used the word _____ instead of another word?	What is another meaning for the word _____?
Do you think the words used in the text help you understand the content better?	How does using the word _____ change the meaning of the text?

Vocabulary Acquisition and Use

The final category for the language standards is entitled Vocabulary Acquisition and Use. There are three anchor standards that fall under this category.

Language Standard 4

The first anchor standard under this category is Language Standard 4, which reads:

Determine or clarify the meaning of unknown and multiple-meaning words and phrases by using context clues, analyzing meaningful word parts, and consulting general and specialized reference materials, as appropriate.

Using context to determine the meaning of unknown words is an important skill to possess. This skill requires the ability to figure out the meaning of unknown words by using the words that surround the unknown word in the sentence.

Take a look at the following sentence:

Jessica was *petrified* of the scary-looking spider on the table.

The unknown word in the sentence is *petrified*. Context clues from the sentence help students figure out that the word *petrified* means scared. You are told that there is a scary-looking spider on the table so you can assume that Jessica is afraid of the spider.

This skill of determining the meaning of words becomes more important to students as they move through the grade levels because they will encounter more complex texts that contain unfamiliar vocabulary. Being able to use context to help determine word meanings is an important skill to hone.

This anchor standard also mentions analyzing word parts. This refers to prefixes, suffixes, and root words. Students can more easily determine the word meaning as they become more familiar with word parts. Have you ever watched a national spelling bee? These kids who participate are masters at this. They ask for word origins and use this knowledge to help spell words that are unfamiliar to them. The following chart breaks down important word parts:

PREFIX: PLACED BEFORE THE BASE WORD. (ADDED TO THE BEGINNING OF A WORD TO MAKE A NEW WORD.)	
Prefix	**Definition**
dis	not
ex	out of
im	not
in	not
min	small
pre	before
un	not
re	do again
SUFFIX: PLACED AFTER THE BASE WORD. (ADDED TO THE END OF A WORD TO MAKE A NEW WORD.)	
Suffix	**Definition**
ed	past (for example, looked)
er	a suffix serving as the regular English formative of agent nouns, being attached to verbs of any origin (for example, laborer)
est	the superlative degree of adjectives and adverbs (for example, biggest)
ful	full of (for example, beautiful)
ing	a suffix of nouns formed from verbs, expressing the action of the verb or its result (for example, running)
ist	person who is (for example, florist)
ly	a suffix forming adverbs from adjectives (for example, gladly)
less	less than (for example, harmless)

Language Standard 5

The second anchor standard in this category is Language Standard 5. Standard 5 reads:

Demonstrate understanding of figurative language, word relationships, and nuances in word meanings.

This anchor delves into going beyond the literal meaning of words and looks at their connotative meanings. Poets are classic examples of authors who use figurative language to convey mood and tone.

This anchor standard can be a bit overwhelming for students. Teachers will have to provide examples of figurative language and discuss its effect on meaning to help students understand how the conveyed meaning of figurative language can be used to interpret an author's intended purpose.

Language Standard 6

The final anchor that falls under the category of vocabulary acquisition and use is Language Standard 6. Standard 6 reads:

> Acquire and use accurately a range of general academic and domain-specific words and phrases sufficient for reading, writing, speaking, and listening at the college and career readiness level; demonstrate independence in gathering vocabulary knowledge when encountering an unknown term important to comprehension or expression.

Vocabulary is very important in the Common Core ELA standards. Students will encounter more complex vocabulary as they encounter more sophisticated texts. They will need to acquire the skills to read and comprehend these high-level vocabulary words, and also use them appropriately in their writing. Helping your child to use the new vocabulary she is learning will be a great way to support her acquisition of the vocabulary words. This can be done by simply having your child use the words in a sentence. The more times she uses the word, the more quickly she will acquire it in her personal vocabulary.

FACT

The National Reading Panel found children learn words indirectly through everyday experiences. Ways to build vocabulary include: 1. Engaging in daily conversation. 2. Listening to adults read. 3. Reading extensively independently.

Basal readers, which were commonly known as readers or reading books, are elementary reading textbooks that teach students to read by combining stories with practice exercises. Basal readers come with individual books for the students, a teacher's edition, and assessments and worksheets.

Basal readers have been used in the United States since the 1830s with the McGuffey Readers. The idea behind basal readers was to have one reading text for each grade level. The Dick and Jane series is one of the most famous basal reading series. Basal reading programs focus on vocabulary instruction to help students comprehend the texts that they read. In the basal series vocabulary is connected to the text that the students are reading. Students complete vocabulary lessons based on the stories and are required to use the vocabulary in and out of the context of the story.

FACT

The Dick and Jane series was produced in the 1950s and 1960s by the Scott Foresman and Company. The series, which was written by William S. Gray and Zerna Sharp, featured Dick and Jane, a little boy and girl who inspired many young readers. The series focused on teaching sight words and had phonetic analysis as a part of each lesson.

Teachers in all subject areas will need to determine the essential vocabulary for their respective content areas in order to help prepare students for the demands of the texts they will encounter. This will mean that they will have to read the texts and determine which vocabulary words are most important for students to know. They will want to focus on vocabulary words that go across content areas (those Tier 2 words that were discussed in Chapter 2).

CHAPTER 8

What Is Expected of Your Kindergarten Student?

Kindergarten is a year of extraordinary growth opportunities for children. They go from being shy learners to confident, self-reflective explorers by the end of the school year. Kindergarten is the building block for a child's future education experiences. In kindergarten, teachers build the foundation for literacy, teach kids to understand the reading and writing connection, and teach about language. This chapter discusses the Common Core ELA standards as they relate to students in kindergarten.

Expectations in Reading

Kindergarten is a foundational year, and it is critical that students leave kindergarten with the early literacy and language skills they need to be confident readers by the end of the 1st grade.

The Common Core ELA standards focus on the primary literacy skills that students need to possess in order to become readers. The standards also concentrate on reading comprehension and the understanding of different text types and genres. Because of the Common Core ELA 50/50 split of reading informational and fictional text in kindergarten, these students are exposed to various writing styles and text types.

Early Literacy Skills

In order for students to learn to read they have to master early literacy skills. These skills should be practiced at home before kindergarten so your child is ready to go. There are twenty-six letters in the English alphabet that, either singularly or combined, make forty-four sounds. (In English, letter combinations can make different sounds other than single letters alone.) A digraph is a single sound, or phoneme, which is pronounced by two letters. For example:

- The diagraph *ch* can be pronounced three different ways. In the word *cherry* it is pronounced *ch*. In the word *Christmas* it is pronounced *k*. In the word *machine*, it is pronounced *sh*.

Learning to read in English can be a challenge. Therefore children need a strong basic understanding of the English sound system so that they can be ready to learn to read. One way to help prepare your child is to ensure she has early literacy skills.

Early literacy skills include:

- Phonological awareness
- Phonemic awareness
- Print awareness

Phonological Awareness

Phonological awareness is the ability to hear word sounds. Phonological awareness includes alliteration, rhyming, and syllabication.

Alliteration is the repeating of consonant sounds at the beginning of a string of words. An example would be the English nursery rhyme "Peter Piper."

Peter Piper picked a peck of pickled peppers.
A peck of pickled peppers Peter Piper picked.
If Peter Piper picked a peck of pickled peppers,
Where's the peck of pickled peppers that Peter Piper picked?

ALERT

If students can't hear the distinct differences in sounds, they will struggle with reading. Practicing phonemic awareness with your child will help her determine the differences in sounds, and will help her become a better reader and speaker.

Phonemic Awareness

Phonemic awareness is similar to phonological awareness, but the focus is on individual sounds. For example, knowing that the letter *b* make the *buh* sound, a phonemic awareness exercise you could try with your child is:

- Say "bat." What sound do you hear at the end? What sound do you hear in the beginning of the word? What sound do you hear in the middle?

Another phonemic activity you can do is to segment phonemes.
- Say "bat" How many sounds do you hear?
- Slowly pronounce the word bat (b/a/t). How many sounds do you hear? (Three.)

Other fun ways to support phonemic awareness include the following:

- Read environmental signs and print. Examples of these might include street signs, labels on food items, and restaurant and store names.

- Play rhyming games by reciting poems and songs. Ask your child if she recognizes which two words rhyme. Dr. Seuss books are wonderful for this activity.
- Word play is another fun way to play with sounds. Say the word "play" then tell your child you are going to take the first sound away. What is the new word? (Lay.)
- Play with picture cards. Ask your child to name each picture and then segment the word into its parts. For example, if your child is looking at the following picture, ask your child what sounds he hears in the word *cat* (k/a/t).

- Play with letter tiles. Help your child use the tiles so that he can make up words and also spell his name.
- Segment words into the word parts as you take a walk. Ask your child to say things that you see in the environment and then segment them into their individual sounds. For example, if you see the following sign, ask your child what sounds she hears in the word *stop* (s/t/o/p).

- Record your child saying letter sounds. This is a way to help him hear the differences that each letter sound makes.

ALERT

Phonological awareness is sometimes confused with phonemic awareness. Remember that *phonemic awareness* is all about hearing word sounds. It is the ability to hear the individual sounds in words and to identify them. *Phonological awareness* is the awareness of words including rhyming words, syllables, and individual sounds.

Print Awareness

Both phonemic and phonological awareness are necessary bridges to decoding written language. It is important that your child master both as he moves into learning to read.

Use the following checklist to assess your child's early literacy development:

Early Literacy Checklist

MY CHILD:
- ❑ Shows an interest in books
- ❑ Makes up stories
- ❑ Knows what a title is
- ❑ Knows what an author is
- ❑ Knows what an illustrator is
- ❑ Retells stories from memory
- ❑ Can turn the pages of a book properly
- ❑ Knows that text reads from top to bottom
- ❑ Knows that when we read and write we start on the left side and move to the right
- ❑ Knows that the illustrations on a page relate to the text
- ❑ Discusses text after reading or being read to
- ❑ Can name rhyming words
- ❑ Reads environmental signs and print (traffic signs, logos, labels)
- ❑ Knows what a letter is

- ❏ Can point out letters in a text
- ❏ Knows the letters of the alphabet
- ❏ Tries to spell words
- ❏ Asks what unknown words say
- ❏ Picks out words he/she knows in a text
- ❏ Can write his/her first and last name
- ❏ Holds a pencil using three fingers
- ❏ Copies letters
- ❏ Copies words

These early literacy skills are essential in preparing your child to be ready for the reading demands of the new Common Core ELA standards.

Practice these skills with your child. Make it playful and game-like. The thing to remember is that children will acquire these skills in their own time. Continuing to model these skills and having your child practice them is the best way to help.

FACT

Phonemic awareness is one of the greatest predictors of future reading success. national literacy assessments like DIBELS and AIMSweb test children on their phonemic awareness to predict their future reading success.

Foundational Skills

The Reading: Foundational Skills standards in the Common Core ELA are the standards that refer to the teaching of reading. The Reading: Foundational Skills standards are only found in grades K–5. They are separated into four categories. Those categories are designed to help students with print concepts, phonological awareness, phonic and word recognition, and fluency.

Teaching reading is very complex. Teachers have to go beyond the standards listed and teach whatever essential early literacy skills are necessary in order for kids to learn to read. There are four Reading: Foundational Skills standards in kindergarten. Standard 1 emphasizes basic features of print including directionality, phonemic awareness, and letter recognition.

Standard 2 emphasizes phonemes and rhyming words. Standard 3 emphasizes phonics and word reading. Standard 4 emphasizes reading texts for understanding. We will go over Reading: Foundational Skills standards 1 and 3 in this section. Included are some activities you can use at home to support these important early literacy skills.

Reading: Foundational Skills Standard 1

The first Reading: Foundational Skills standard in kindergarten reads:

Demonstrate understanding of the organization and basic features of print.
a. Follow words from left to right, top to bottom, and page by page.
b. Recognize that spoken words are represented in written language by specific sequences of letters.
c. Understand that words are separated by spaces in print.
d. Recognize and name all uppercase and lowercase letters of the alphabet.

As you can see, there are many sub-skills listed that kindergarten students are expected to master.

ESSENTIAL

One way to help your child recognize and name all the uppercase and lowercase letters is to get alphabet letter flashcards that exhibit both uppercase and lowercase letters. Help your child go through the letter cards.

There are some awesome online alphabet game sites that help kids learn their letters. Here are a couple to try:

- *www.learnenglish.org.uk/kids/antics/index.html*
- *www.abcya.com*

Print Concepts

Students must know how to hold a book. They must know how to follow the words from left to right and top to bottom. They must understand that letters represent sounds, which represent words. All of these foundational print concept skills fall under Reading: Foundational Skills Standard 1.

These print concept skills should be modeled by reading with your child so as to ensure that she is comfortable interacting with print. Here are some quick tips to use to help your child grasp print concepts:

- Show your child the title and author on texts that you read. As you read a book point to the text and say, "The title of this book is _____." "The author of the book is _____." As you continue to model this your child will internalize the meaning.
- Teach your child book-handling skills. Teach your child that the book opens to the right, and demonstrate how to flip the pages from front to back. Teachers model this when using big books, but you can do the same thing at home with a regular book.
- Teach your child directionality by pointing to words as you read. Tell your child to notice that when we read we go from left to right on the page.
- Talk about the letters, words, and sentences on the page. Tell your child that letters form words, which form sentences. An easy way to demonstrate this is to write a few sentences from a book on a piece of paper. Have your child circle the letters, words, and sentences.
- Talk about the fact that words have spaces between them. You can model this by showing your child the spaces in a book, and then writing the words on paper and explicitly pointing out the spaces to your child.
- Label objects in your house by using sticky notes. You can label a door, window, chair, table, and so on. By labeling these objects you provide a print-rich environment, which will help your child build foundational reading skills.
- Reinforce alphabet recognition of both the uppercase and lowercase letters. You can buy an alphabet chart or write the alphabet on paper, make an alphabet book, and play alphabet recognition games using signs and other environmental print.

The foundational skills in kindergarten also focus on phonological awareness. As discussed in the section on early literacy skills, phonological awareness is a precursory skill to reading. These are all the fun skills that kids practice when reciting nursery rhymes and reciting poetry. These skills can be further supported for your kindergartner by playing phonological games like the following:

- **Finish the rhyme:** Start a rhyme and have your child finish it. For example, the cat was very _____ (fat). As your child finishes the rhyme talk about why the words *cat* and *fat* rhyme.
- **Counting games:** Have your child count the number of words in a sentence. You can model this by holding up a finger for each word as you dictate a sentence aloud.
- **Make a new word:** Play a game where you change the ending and beginning sounds in familiar words to make new words. For example, *man* and *can*; or *bat* and *fat*. In this case you are changing the initial sound.

Make the foundational skills practice fun for your child. These essential skills must be mastered as children continue to grow in their literacy development.

Reading: Foundational Skills Standard 3

Reading: Foundational Skills Standard 3 reads:

Know and apply grade-level phonics and word analysis skills in decoding words.
a. Demonstrate basic knowledge of letter-sound correspondences by producing the primary or most frequent sound for each consonant.
b. Associate the long and short sounds with the common spellings (graphemes) for the five major vowels.
c. Read common high-frequency words by sight (e.g., the, of, to, you, she, my, is, are, do, does).
d. Distinguish between similarly spelled words by identifying the sounds of the letters that differ.

Learning sight words is critical in early grades. Sight words do not require sounding out and can be read as a whole. They are high-frequency words that kids need to recognize quickly. In addition to the words cited by the Common Core authors, other examples include: *said, it, he.*

ALERT

You can get a copy of the sight words or high-frequency words from your child's teacher.

Note that the two terms (*sight words* and *high-frequency words*) might be used interchangeably by your child's teacher. Practice sight words with your child so that she can get them into her memory bank and read these words without effort.

ESSENTIAL

For more information on activities to support kindergarten foundational skills you can visit these websites: *www.pbskids.org* and *www.starfall.com.*

Literature

Kindergarten students should be exposed to ample amounts of fiction to learn about the structures of literary text. There are nine Reading Literature standards in the Common Core ELA standards document. This chapter will explore Reading: Literature Standards 1, 2, and 3. These standards focus on understanding key details in a text and story elements like characters, settings, and events. These are all essential for comprehension.

Reading: Literature Standard 1

The Reading: Literature standard 1 reads:

With prompting and support, ask and answer questions about key details in a text.

Many of the standards in kindergarten use the verbiage, "with prompting and support." This is important to note because, as you might recall, the Common Core standards have raised the bar in expectations. Thus, children will need adequate support to comprehend the higher levels of text that they will encounter.

Asking and answering questions about the text and using the text in the response is something that must be modeled to young children. Modeling helps children internalize a concept and eventually utilize it in their own work.

Read Aloud

Reading aloud to your child is an effective way to model using text-based evidence. Find a book that has a conflict that is solved by the end of the story. Read the story and talk aloud about the actions and events that help solve the conflict. There are many great children's storybooks with conflicts in them. Both the Clifford and Franklin book series always have great storylines with great resolutions at the end.

Reading: Literature Standard 2

Reading: Literature standard 2 calls for students to retell familiar stories. The standard reads:

With prompting and support, retell familiar stories, including key details.

Notice that the importance of retelling and including key details is reiterated. As you might recall from Chapter 4, Key Ideas and Details is one of the anchor standards. All of these standards relate to teaching students to identify key ideas from texts. Following is a key details chart you can share with your child. This chart can be used as a basis for discussion when you are reading aloud with your child.

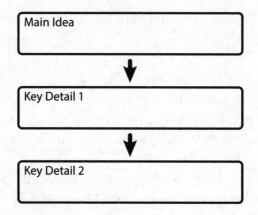

Main Idea

Key Detail 1

Key Detail 2

Reading: Literature Standard 3

Reading: Literature standard 3 reads:

With prompting and support, identify characters, settings, and major events in a story.

Ask your child about the characters in the stories you read. Have him talk about their actions and how they look. Do the same thing with setting. Discuss where the story takes place and if the setting changes. Finally, talk about the events in the story. Ask your child how these events affect the characters and the final resolution.

Informational Text

Because of the Common Core, kindergarten students will be exposed to more informational or nonfiction text than students had been years ago. In the past, a kindergarten teacher might only read nonfiction texts when celebrating holidays like Presidents' Day or Martin Luther King Day. For the most part teachers focused on reading fictional stories, and the students would write mainly narratives or stories. At that time most nonfiction books were typically written at a Lexile level that was too difficult for children of this age group. Today many publishers have nonfiction texts written at the pre-primer level.

FACT

The Common Core requires a 50/50 split of fictional and informational text for kindergartners. This means that children begin learning about the text structures of nonfiction at an early age.

Making Connections

Reading: Informational Text standard 3 reads:

With prompting and support, describe the connection between two individuals, events, ideas, or pieces of information in a text.

This standard requires that your child discuss information gained from more than one nonfiction text. For example, if your child is learning about life cycles, she may read about the life cycle of a butterfly and the life cycle of a frog. Students will discuss the similarities between both life cycles and the differences. You can practice this at home with your child by discussing connections between events and ideas that you encounter.

How to Support the Reading: Informational Text Standard

Young children love informational texts because such works are a window to their world. Kindergarten-age children are very inquisitive and are natural explorers. Some great tips to support informational text reading include:

- Read nonfiction texts to your child. There are many nonfiction pieces with good storylines. Biographies are always a good bet.
- Talk about timelines with your child after reading a biography. Explain how timelines help us see visually how time passes.
- Create a timeline with your child about her life.
- Talk about the illustrations, labels, and graphics in nonfiction texts. Explain their purpose to your child.
- Create illustrations and graphics for a nonfiction text that you and your child create. This is a fun way to practice the skills you just reviewed.

CHAPTER 9

Expectations in Kindergarten Writing

Expressing an opinion in writing is a skill that is taught in kindergarten. In kindergarten, students can write about their favorite and least favorite topics, ideas, and items. They can write about what interests them the most and express opinions using pictures and sentence frames to formulate opinions. The kids are connected to the subject matter because they are experts on it, and that helps them foster a feeling of success. This chapter will explore writing standards of the Common Core for kindergarten. These standards are separated into four categories: Text types and purposes, production and distribution of writing, research to build and present knowledge, and range of writing.

Text Types and Purposes

The following standards relate to teaching students to write for different purposes. Students in kindergarten become familiar with the three different writing genres (argument, informational/explanatory, and narrative) as they practice writing in these genres. This section will focus on writing standards 1 and 3.

If your child struggles with discussing opinions, provide sentence frames and share your own ideas. The more he hears these models, the more natural it will be for him to use them.

Writing Standard 1

Writing standard 1 reads:

Use a combination of drawing, dictating, and writing to compose opinion pieces in which they tell a reader the topic or the name of the book they are writing about and state an opinion or preference about the topic or book (e.g., My favorite book is . . .).

The standard notes that students may use drawings to represent their ideas. This is important because a lot of the primary texts these students encounter use pictures to provide clues to figure out unfamiliar words. These texts also teach kids that illustrations and pictures relate to the words on the page. Allowing kindergarten children to express their ideas using pictures is an important developmental process that should be cultivated.

Sentence frames can be used to give children the language needed to express opinions. Examples include: My favorite book is _____. My least favorite toy is _____.

Reacting to Text

The final standard under the category of Text Types and Purposes is writing standard 3. Writing standard 3 reads:

Use a combination of drawing, dictating, and writing to narrate a single event or several loosely linked events, tell about the events in the order in which they occurred, and provide a reaction to what happened.

The last part of the standard notes that kids should provide a reaction to what happens in the text. This is an important skill that should be modeled for kindergarten children. This skill involves reading closely to develop an opinion about what is happening in a text. It requires that your child begin to critically think about the characters and events and connect those experiences with her own. Typical reactions may include being happy that an event occurred. Continue to talk to your child when reading and ask for an opinion on what she read. Take it a step further by having her write about or draw her reaction.

Sequencing Events

Students in kindergarten should begin to understand that stories have a beginning, middle, and end. They should begin to incorporate this in their own writing, and also recognize how to write about events that they read about in sequential order. Writing standard 3 asks kids to recall what happened in a story in sequential order and to react to it. This is quite sophisticated for kindergarten children. They often struggle with remembering the sequence of events in stories if they have not read them numerous times. To help support this standard at home, teach your child to note what is happening in the stories that he reads. Use the following sequencing chart to help.

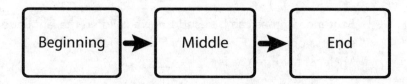

Sequencing is a skill that crosses content areas. Your child will sequence numbers in math, events in history, and tell story sequences. Continue supporting this important skill at home.

Text and Picture Writing

Using pictures to convey meaning is another key component to help students develop their writing skills. The use of pictures is modeled by bringing students' attention to illustrations in a text and showing them the relationship that illustrations have to the words on the page.

Text and picture writing can develop as follows:

ilb
Beginning stages

I lic the br.
Middle stages

I lik the bird.
Fluent stages

Students in the beginning stages are not paying attention to capitalization or punctuation. There is no line spacing between the words, and the students are only writing the first letter sound.

Students in the middle stages are putting spaces between the words and are paying attention to punctuation. They are spelling the high-frequency word "the."

Students growing to the fluent level have a grasp on the high-frequency words and are using their knowledge of phonics to sound out unknown words. The word "like" is misspelled, but you can see that the child is hearing the beginning, middle, and ending sounds in the word. The silent *e* is left off, which is typical for beginning readers and writers.

ESSENTIAL

Be patient as your child progresses through the stages of writing. Each stage is important and has to be mastered before moving to the next step.

Here is an example of the stages of writing:

DRAWING
- Drawings should represent the story
- Drawings should have details to support the story

SCRIBBLING
- Scribbles are used to represent letters
- Should begin to include some letters as the child progresses

LETTER-LIKE FORMS
- Are letter-like formations, but are invented by the child
- Represent letters the child has seen in print and is trying to mimic drawing

RANDOM LETTERS OR LETTER STRINGS
- Strings of letters written randomly on the page
- Student may include words he knows, including his name
- No letter and sound connections; words are written randomly

INVENTED SPELLING

- Child uses knowledge of word sounds to try to spell words
- May write the word *cat* as *kaat*; in this example, the child hears the sounds in the word and writes them on the page

QUESTION

Why is drawing important in kindergarten writing?
As students develop as writers the drawings and figures they include in their writing help create meaning for their stories. It also teaches students to use picture clues when they are reading texts to increase comprehension.

CONVENTIONAL SPELLING

- Words are spelled correctly

An alphabet chart (like the following) is a great tool that your child can reference as he is writing.

Aa	Bb	Cc	Dd
Ee	Ff	Gg	Hh
Ii	Jj	Kk	Ll
Mm	Nn	Oo	Pp
Qq	Rr	Ss	Tt
Uu	Vv	Ww	Xx
Yy	Zz		

Your child's teacher may also have a word wall in the classroom with frequently spelled words. This is a useful tool to help your child begin to spell words correctly. Do not worry if your child is using inventive spelling. This is encouraged because it is a necessary stage of development as children are learning to connect sounds and words.

Production and Distribution of Writing

As kindergarten students move through the writing stages they are asked to work with peers and the teacher to edit their writing. Editing is an important skill that needs to be cultivated starting in kindergarten.

The writing standards call for students to work collaboratively to accept suggestions from peers. This can be tricky when working with young children. Again, these skills have to be modeled by adults and a tool such as a rubric must be used to help students determine what is expected.

Writing Rubrics

Writing rubrics are documents that provide guidelines for students on what is expected in their writing. Your child's teacher should have a rubric that your child can use to determine how she is doing in her writing. This rubric can also serve as a guide for peer reviews or collaborations.

Writing standard 5 reads:

With guidance and support from adults, respond to questions and suggestions from peers and add details to strengthen writing as needed.

ALERT

Rubrics provide specific details on student mastery. They are excellent tools for assessment. However, rubrics become useless if they are not used consistently to address growth.

Starting in kindergarten, students will be asked to use the peer editing process to improve their writing. This is done with teacher support and guidance. You can help your child become familiar with the editing process by introducing rubrics at home.

Here is a sample rubric that you can use at home with your child:

My writing makes sense.	Yes	No
I used punctuation marks.	Yes	No
I used capital letters.	Yes	No

I have a finger space between words.	Yes	No
I sounded out my words.	Yes	No

Here is another example rubric:

I have a capital at the beginning on my sentences?	🙁	🙂
The man is tall.		
I put a space between the words?	🙁	🙂
The man is tall.		
I used punctuation to end my sentences?	🙁	🙂
The man is tall.		
My picture matches my words?	🙂	🙂
The man is tall.		

Using a rubric with your child can help him understand and internalize the expectations in writing. You can also practice peer editing by having your child complete the rubric on a writing piece that you write.

Nonfiction Writing

Students enjoy writing narrative texts. This includes stories, letters, and poetry. Writing standard 2 asks students to write informative texts. Standard 2 reads:

Use a combination of drawing, dictating, and writing to compose informative/explanatory texts in which they name what they are writing about and supply some information about the topic.

Developing the skills to compose informative/explanatory texts involves students becoming familiar with the text features of this style of writing. You can have your child write a simple report on his favorite animal. Be sure that your child includes important facts and illustrations to help the reader understand the text.

Another activity that is useful for kindergarten students is to have them write a recipe. They have to explain the steps in making the item. Here is a recipe card template you can use with your child:

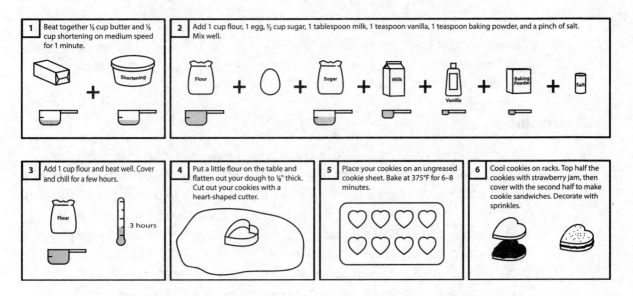

Research to Build and Present Knowledge

Students in kindergarten are introduced to research writing. Writing standard 7 reads:

Participate in shared research and writing projects (e.g., explore a number of books by a favorite author and express opinions about them).

Reading multiple books on a single subject or by a single author and then writing an opinion piece is a wonderful way to support this standard. This is a great activity to teach kids the value of research. There are so many wonderful authors out there with some fabulous books. Teachers could perhaps have kids read Cinderella stories by different authors and then write about their favorite version of the story, using material from the text.

ESSENTIAL

You can support this standard at home by having your child write about different movie series, and then talk about her favorite. Additionally, your child can compare different games she plays and express which one is her favorite.

This standard calls for guidance and support, so offering suggestions regarding what to compare and how to form an opinion are good modeling techniques that you can provide your child.

Technology

Children are expected to use technology to communicate in writing starting in kindergarten. This requires that students in kindergarten begin to learn basic computer skills like keyboarding and how to log on to a computer. This section will explore digital writing and the importance of handwriting in kindergarten. Writing standard 6 reads:

> With guidance and support from adults, explore a variety of digital tools to produce and publish writing, including in collaboration with peers.

This is a huge shift from what has been the norm in kindergarten. Most schools are beginning to provide digital technologies to their students, meaning that even kindergarten children are using the Internet as an online research tool.

To support this standard at home you can have your child go to some kindergarten-friendly websites to search for information on different topics. These sites include:

- *www.bbckids.ca*
- *www.enchantedlearning.com/Home.html*
- *ecokids.ca/pub/kids_home.cfm*
- *kids.nationalgeographic.com*

Range of Writing

Writing in kindergarten is very important, and we cannot leave the subject without discussing handwriting. The Common Core expresses a push for digital technology and teaching children keyboarding skills. However, this chapter would be remiss if it did not include a note about the connection between handwriting and reading development.

FACT

Here is a great website to help demonstrate proper pencil grip: *http://k1ac.weebly.com/parent-education/pencil-grip*.

Handwriting improves fine motor development and creative writing skills. Handwriting is also necessary because in many classrooms note taking is done without access to a computer. Handwriting is also a good way to teach and reinforce the letters of the alphabet, especially when students say the letters as they form them by hand.

CHAPTER 10

Expectations in Kindergarten Speaking, Listening, and Language

Kindergarten teachers work hard to help students express their ideas and feelings. Events like "Show and Tell" and "Student of the Week" are examples of how teachers encourage conversations in the classroom. Activities like these offer opportunities for kids to talk about themselves, their interests, and their friends and family. As the teacher guides oral presentations like these, all students meanwhile learn the importance of active listening and taking turns speaking. The authors of the Common Core included these skills because they want students to collaborate and have the ability to effectively communicate orally as they move through the grade levels. This chapter explores the speaking and listening standards for kindergarten, discusses how the standards impact the classroom, and talks about how you can support them at home.

Comprehension and Collaboration

As the title suggests, comprehension and collaboration are the focus of the first set of standards in speaking and listening. There are six Speaking and Listening Standards in kindergarten. These standards focus on the interpersonal skills of collaboration and emphasize public speaking. This section will cover several speaking and listening standards by providing simple activities you can do at home to support their development.

Speaking and Listening Standard 1

Speaking and Listening standard 1 reads:

Participate in collaborative conversations with diverse partners about kindergarten topics and texts with peers and adults in small and larger groups.
a. Follow agreed-upon rules for discussions (e.g., listening to others and taking turns speaking about the topics and texts under discussion).
b. Continue a conversation through multiple exchanges.

Learning the rules of conversation is a very important skill that kindergarten students must learn in order to be successful throughout grade school and beyond. These skills do not come easy, as many children are not aware of the specific rules in formal conversation. In fact, younger children often have difficulty comprehending the idea of taking turns, be it taking turns in line to get a drink of water or taking turns to be the line leader. Let's face it, kindergarten children can be a little egocentric, and so teaching specific rules for collaboration is a good first step in preparing them to become collaborative.

Speaking and listening skills have to be modeled and practiced in order for students to understand them. Some of the key skills to model for speaking and listening are:

SPEAKING SKILLS
- Did you keep your eyes on the audience?
- Did you stay on topic?

- Did you speak loud enough?
- Did you speak clearly?

LISTENING SKILLS
- Did you keep your eyes on the speaker?
- Did you sit still?
- Did you listen to the speaker?

Using lists like this to provide behavioral guidance for kindergarten-age students is a good strategy to use. You can use pictures to represent the behaviors you desire or you can make up hand motions. The idea is to make it relevant so that your child can grasp the concepts.

Again, it's important to remember that kids learn best by seeing and then doing. Model good listening and speaking for your child, and then discuss the behavior. You can model how you talk with your banker, for example, or a family member. These soft skills are essential to prepare children for the speaking and listening tasks they will be asked to perform in later grades and beyond.

ESSENTIAL

Many children struggle with staying on topic. Have visual cues to remind your child to stay on task.

Continuing a Conversation

As a reminder, the last part of the speaking and listening standard 1 reads:

Continue a conversation through multiple exchanges.

This is a skill that can be modeled by asking your child follow-up questions about a topic. You can start by posing a question and then having your child respond. You will in turn respond and ask another question. This will teach your child about continuing conversations on the same topic. More than likely, this activity will already be taking place in your child's classroom when the class discusses key ideas in books or talks about topics or events. Learning to stay on topic is an important precursory skill. It is also an important speaking skill because students will have to learn how to participate in group exchanges prior to entering college and the workplace.

Asking for Clarification

The ability to obtain information from multiple sources is a skill that begins in kindergarten. Speaking and Listening standard 2 reads:

> Confirm understanding of a text read aloud or information presented orally or through other media by asking and answering questions about key details and requesting clarification if something is not understood.

This standard asks that students begin to ask and answer questions about key details in texts and other media sources. In addition, it asks students to seek clarification on points they do not understand. You can help model this at home by watching informational videos and asking your child questions about what he saw. Here are some questions to consider asking:

- What was the video mainly about?
- What were the most important ideas in the video?
- How did the video help you understand the subject of _____ better?
- What questions do you still have about the subject after watching the video?

FACT

The Florida Center for Reading Research has some great resources on questioning strategies. The following web links can be a useful resource: *www.fcrr.org/assessment/ET/routines/pdf/instRoutines_KC2 .pdf, www.fcrr.org/assessment/ET/routines/pdf/instRoutines_KAHLQ .pdf, www.fcrr.org/assessment/ET/questions/QTGK/quesKComp.html.*

Presentation of Knowledge and Ideas

You may notice that your child is asked to give a public presentation in class starting in kindergarten. Allowing your child to practice public speaking at home or in a club or church setting is a great way to help build this important skill set.

Speaking and Listening: Relevant Details

Describing familiar people, places, and events is the aim of the skills under the umbrella of Presentation of Knowledge and Ideas. Students in kindergarten use their listening comprehension to gain knowledge that they then present orally. This means that students will be asked to listen to gain understanding so they can then collaboratively discuss their learning and present their understanding.

Being able to present information and ideas clearly while including supporting details is the aim of Speaking and Listening standard 4. This standard asks students to express their ideas clearly by including relevant details. Speaking and Listening Standard 4 reads:

Describe familiar people, places, things, and events and, with prompting and support, provide additional detail.

Supporting details can be easily taught to kindergarten children by using an adjectives chart. Show your child different objects and have her answer the questions that relate to the object on the adjectives chart.

- What does it smell like? _____
- What does it look like? _____
- What does it taste like? _____
- What does it feel like? _____
- What does it sound like? _____

Take the answers and have your child include them when she speaks about the object. You should first model how to do it using a familiar object.

Complete Sentences

Speaking and Listening standard 6 reads:

Speak audibly and express thoughts, feelings, and ideas clearly.

This standard calls for teaching students to speak in a clear voice so the audience can understand clearly what is being expressed. Often students in kindergarten need help with remembering to speak in whole sentences. Remind your child and correct her when she does not use complete sentences when talking.

Speaking in complete sentences is an important skill that kindergarten children must master. Many students in kindergarten struggle with speaking clearly, because they do not speak in clear and complete sentences. The first step in understanding this standard at the kindergarten level is to explain what a complete sentence is.

Teach your child that a complete sentence represents a complete thought. You can show him examples of complete sentences in writing. You can also teach complete sentences by correcting your child when he uses an incomplete sentence. You want to correct positively and share the correct way to say the sentence. Don't just tell him that he said it incorrectly; tell him why it was incorrect and model the correct way to say it in a complete sentence.

FACT

Throughout the kindergarten standards the term "with guidance and support" is repeatedly mentioned. Guidance and support refers to the importance of modeling behaviors for primary-age children. Many of the tasks that your child will be asked to attempt in the primary grades are there to serve as a model for skills that will soon become independent as your child grows older, and the practice becomes developmentally appropriate for his age level.

Modeling is a concrete way to show the behavior that you expect from children. It is very effective because children are very observant and repeat behaviors they see. That is why we always emphasize the importance of having positive models for children since they are very impressionable. How many times has your child come home repeating something she heard at school or at a friend's house? Throughout this book you will find language frames and checklists that you can use to model desired literacy behaviors for your child.

Conventions

Language standards are crucial in kindergarten. Students must learn about the language system, including our alphabet system as well as the rules of spoken language. Skills students learn include things like having the ability to print all uppercase and lowercase letters and using varied parts of speech correctly. The grammar, speech, and vocabulary skills span across all content areas as students will need to communicate their ideas in writing and orally. The language standards play a large part in the kindergarten curriculum and have to be taught within the context of teaching reading, writing, and speaking and listening.

We are used to conventions that refer to spelling, capitalization, and punctuation. These skills are listed under language standard 2. Again, these are taught during the teaching of reading and writing.

Writing Conventions

Understanding the importance of writing conventions is a skill that begins in kindergarten. Students will be introduced to the importance of looking at their writing to see if they have included basic grammar conventions like capitals, ending punctuation, and spacing between words. Using a checklist can be a great way to reinforce basic writing conventions for your child. Here is a sample checklist for writing conventions you can use with your kindergartner:

- ❑ I used capitals
- ❑ I used periods
- ❑ I put my name on my paper
- ❑ I have spaces between my words
- ❑ I spelled sight words correctly

Teaching Nouns and Pronouns

Kindergarten students should be familiar with nouns and pronouns. A noun is any word that names a person, place, or thing. Your child should have a firm grasp on what a noun is. You can practice this by providing your child with a picture like the following one.

Have him name all the nouns he can find in the picture.

Remember that pronouns stand for nouns. They are words like "he," "she," "they," and "we." You can do a pronoun sort with your child to reinforce this concept:

MATERIALS:
- Index cards with the following words: he, you, they, it, I, us, sit, hit, run, camp
- 1 sheet of paper
- Writing utensils

PROCEDURE:

1. Take a sheet of paper and draw a line in the middle.
2. On one side write a header that says, "Pronouns."
3. On the other side write a header that says, "Not a Pronoun."
4. Ask your child to place the cards on the correct side.
5. As you read the cards together, ask your child why he thinks it is or is not a pronoun.

Mr. Space Man

Kindergarten teachers across America use the term "Mr. Space Man" to represent the spacing between words in sentences. This can be referred to as a finger space. You can have your child model this by giving her a piece of lined paper or by using the following lines. Have your child write words on it, ensuring that she puts a finger on the page to indicate the space needed between the words.

The   bag   is   brown.

_____

_____

_____

_____

_____

_____

_____

_____

_____

_____

_____

_____

Sight Words

There are many sight word sheets that are out there. A sight word is a word that is frequently found in reading: Words like "the," "a," "at," and "house" are considered sight words. You can practice these with your child. Be sure your child not only can read the sight words but also can write them and use them in writing. You can obtain a sight word list from your child's teacher.

QUESTION

Where can I find other sight word lists?
Two of the most popular sight word lists are the Dolch list and Fry's list. The following websites provide both the Dolch and Fry's list: *http://bogglesworldesl.com/dolch/lists.htm, www.uniqueteachingresources.com/support-files/fryfirst100set.pdf.*

Support Activities

The kindergarten standards are very robust and require a lot of scaffolding and support. Here are some practice activities to help your child master some of the basic skills she will need in kindergarten.

READ THE FOLLOWING TEXT ALOUD TO YOUR CHILD:

There once lived a little boy named Joseph. Joseph liked to run in the forest with his pet dog named Sam. One day while running in the forest Joseph and Sam were met by a large grizzly bear. At first they were frightened, but soon found that the bear was very kind and warm. He welcomed them to his borough and introduced them to his cubs. Joseph and Sam become forever friends with Bear and his cubs.

QUESTIONS TO ASK:
- What is the story mainly about?
- Why were Joseph and Sam afraid of Bear at first?
- What did Bear do to show he was kind?

PUT THE SENTENCES IN THE CORRECT ORDER.

1. . is The white cat
2. 5 am years I . old
3. like . We go to school to

ANSWER THE FOLLOWING:

1. What words can you think of to describe the sun?
2. What words can you think of to describe an apple?
3. What words can you think of to describe an orange?
4. What words can you think of to describe yourself?
5. Write a story about a friend. Be sure to use describing words.

READ THE FOLLOWING POEMS TO YOUR CHILD:

The sun is yellow
The moon is white
I like them both for day and night.
My cat is soft
My dog is not
Each of them I cannot live without.

1. Ask your child how the two poems are alike.
2. Ask your child to use evidence from the text in her answer.

Activity: Sentence Completion

MATERIALS NEEDED:

- Kindergarten-ruled paper with a space to draw
- Word-card words (see following)
- Sticky notes
- Pencils and crayons

PROCEDURE:

1. Copy the words to make word cards; you can use sticky notes or index cards cut in half for the words
2. Mix the word cards up
3. Have your child put the words in order to make a complete sentence
4. After she has made her complete sentence give her a sheet of paper and the writing utensils
5. Tell her to copy the words for her sentence on the sheet of paper
6. Remind her to use spaces between the words
7. Tell your child to illustrate the sentence using details

WORD-CARD WORDS:									
The	dog	and	the	cat	are	in	the	tall	grass.

CHAPTER 11

What Is Expected of Your 1st Grade Student?

First grade is the year students learn to read. Students should leave 1st grade with an ability to read grade-appropriate material fluently with comprehension. Breaking that reading code can be a challenge for some students, but with patience and good teaching strategies all kids can learn to read. The authors of the Common Core ELA standards have placed a strong focus on Reading: Foundational Skills standards in the 1st grade. The standards emphasize how essential this grade level is in ensuring that kids have received the reading instruction they need in order to meet the increased demand of the reading literature and information standards. This chapter will go over some essential 1st grade reading standards and the impact they have on instruction. The standards covered in this chapter represent the essential reading skills needed for your 1st grader to meet the needs of the Common Core ELA standards. Skills highlighted include reading fluency, phonics instruction, and reading comprehension.

Expectations in Reading

During 1st grade, students are taught to read fluently. Phonics skills are mastered and students should leave 1st grade with a firm grasp on decoding. Decoding is the ability to use letter and sound relationships to translate a series of symbols (letters) into a word with meaning.

FACT

Fluency refers to the rate and prosody, or intonation and rhythmic aspect of language, in reading. Reading fluently is directly related to comprehension. Students who read fluently comprehend texts more readily than their peers who do not read fluently.

When you think about it, learning to read is truly a complex activity. Children must first understand that letters make up sounds, which become words. They have to recognize and know the sounds for each of these letters. They must blend those sounds together to make words. They must then make meaning of those words. This process starts in kindergarten with all the focus on building literacy foundations.

The Common Core ELA standards have raised the bar, because students are also responsible for higher comprehension skills while wrestling with increased Lexile levels.

ESSENTIAL

The Lexile band in grade 1 spans from 250–300. This means that students in 1st grade will encounter texts in this Lexile span. Some books in the 250–300 range include *Anansi the Spider*, The *Girl Who Cried Monster*, *Nate the Great Goes Undercover,* and *The Cow That Went Oink*.

As a parent you may notice that your child is asked to respond to complex texts in written form along with speaking and listening tasks. This is an exciting change that also presents increased demands for students. It is imperative that your child is reading at home and that you are supporting his ability to read texts that are grade-level texts. Phonics instruction is particularly important in the 1st grade. All of these foundational skills help students leave 1st grade reading on grade level.

Reading at an Appropriate Level

One way to help your child read books at an appropriate level is to apply the "just right rule." To check if a book is just right for your child, use the following scale.

TOO EASY
- I know all the words in the book
- I can read the book very quickly
- I have read this book many times
- I can retell the story easily

JUST RIGHT
- I know most of the words in the book
- I understand what I am reading
- I can figure out what I don't understand
- I can tell someone what I read

TOO HARD
- I don't understand a lot of the words in the book
- I forget information that I am reading
- It is confusing
- I am reading very slowly
- I cannot retell what I have read

Early Literacy Skills

The phonics skills taught in grade 1 pick up where kindergarten left off. The most basic phonics skills are taught in kindergarten, and then in grade 1 the skills become a bit more complex. There are four Reading: Foundational Skills standards in 1st grade. They fall under the categories of print concepts, phonological awareness, phonics and word recognition, and fluency.

FACT

The key functions of reading require students to read text in order to comprehend. Students in 1st grade are asked to read decodable texts and respond to comprehension questions about what they are reading. Help your child with this by asking her about what she read.

By the end of 1st grade, children are able to easily decode one-syllable words and decode two-syllable words following basic patterns by breaking the words into parts. First graders also read words with inflectional endings and recognize and read grade-appropriate irregularly spelled words.

Print Concepts

Print concepts continue to build in the 1st grade. At this grade level students continue to build fluency by recognizing the features of a sentence, including the first word, capitalization, and ending punctuation. Reading: Foundational Skills standard 1 reads:

Demonstrate understanding of the organization and basic features of print.
a. Recognize the distinguishing features of a sentence (e.g., first word, capitalization, ending punctuation).

"Sentence Builders" is a great activity for reinforcing this concept with your 1st grader. Here is how to play:

MATERIALS NEEDED:
- Picture cards with different activities

- Writing paper
- Writing utensils

PROCEDURE:

1. Provide your child with picture cards, which will serve as sentence starters.
2. Ask your child to construct a sentence about the picture.
3. Have him tell you the sentence aloud.
4. Have him dictate the sentence on paper.
5. Be sure to remind him to use capitalization and ending punctuation.

Making sure your child is comfortable with print concepts is important, as these skills will also be expected in his writing. Continuing to point out sentences and talking about their punctuation is a nice way to keep this skill fresh.

Phonological Awareness

Phonological awareness continues in the 1st grade. Remember, phonological awareness refers to the global awareness of speech. This includes onset and rhyme, syllabication, blending, and segmenting sounds. According to the standard, students are expected to demonstrate an understanding of spoken words, syllables, and sounds. Reading: Foundational Skills standard 2 reads:

Demonstrate understanding of spoken words, syllables, and sounds (phonemes).
a. Distinguish long from short vowel sounds in spoken single-syllable words.
b. Orally produce single-syllable words by blending sounds (phonemes), including consonant blends.
c. Isolate and pronounce initial, medial vowel, and final sounds (phonemes) in spoken single-syllable words.
d. Segment spoken single-syllable words into their complete sequence of individual sounds (phonemes).

Wordplay is very important for helping 1st graders learn to read. Poetry and songs are a great way to encourage your child's ear for sounds, and improve her ability to play with words. To assist with this at home, try the following phonological awareness activities:

Sounds Substitution

Have your child change the beginning sounds in a familiar song like "Row, row, row your boat."

Instead of singing "row, row, row your boat" you can replace the initial sound of *r* with an *s* and sing "sow, sow, sow your soat." This is a fun way to play with sounds substitution.

Segmenting

Give your child words to segment. You can use the words on the following list as a starting point. Tell your child to say each syllable as she repeats the word:

word	segments
water	w/a/t/e/r or wa/ter
from	f/r/o/m
set	s/e/t
had	h/a/d
man	m/a/n

Alliteration

Have your child create her own tongue twister. ("Silly Sally sang songs sending Sam sailing.")

Manipulation

This activity has to do with adding and deleting sounds and syllables.

Deleting

Have your child take the first sound off of the following words:

Sam	Am
Fan	An
Map	Ap
Rope	Ope
Park	Ark

Adding

Have your child add beginning sounds or endings to words. For example, have your child add "-ing" to the following words:

Run	Running
Sun	Sunning
Firm	Firming
Scram	Scramming
Fan	Fanning

Phonics Instruction

Phonics instruction continues in the 1st grade. Reading: Foundational Skills standard 3 reads:

Know and apply grade-level phonics and word analysis skills in decoding words.

a. Know the spelling-sound correspondences for common consonant digraphs.

b. Decode regularly spelled one-syllable words.

c. Know final -e and common vowel team conventions for representing long vowel sounds.

d. Use knowledge that every syllable must have a vowel sound to determine the number of syllables in a printed word.

e. Decode two-syllable words following basic patterns by breaking the words into syllables.

f. Read words with inflectional endings.

g. Recognize and read grade-appropriate irregularly spelled words.

Digraphs

Digraphs are two letters that make one sound. For instance, *sh, ch, wh,* and *th* are all digraphs. Your child should be able to decode these words without trying to sound out each sound. He should automatically know that it is a digraph and makes one sound. You can have your child sort word cards into their respective digraph category. For instance, you can use a picture of a ship, chips, whistle, and thorn. Your child would then sort the pictures into the correct digraph category.

Another activity to support this is to have your child read words with consonant digraphs. You can create stories of word lists using digraphs. Notice if your child is trying to sound the digraphs out. If he is, remind him that it is a digraph and has one sound.

Long Vowel e

Students in 1st grade should be able to fluently read words with the long vowel e sound. Some teachers call it the magic e, because when an e is at the end of the word it makes the vowel say its own name. Examples of the long vowel silent e are: *bike, like, hike,* and *spike.*

You can find books at the library with the long vowel silent e pattern. Check the decodable books section. Your librarian should be able to help you find these books. Practice reading words with long vowel silent e with your child. Talk about the rule as you read the words.

Here are some websites with long vowel silent e activities as well as some videos to reinforce the concept:

- *www.kizphonics.com/phonics/long-o-silent-e-phonics-games*
- *www.starfall.com/n/skills/silent-e/play.htm*
- *www.fun4thebrain.com/English/magice.html*
- *www.starfall.com/n/long-a/la/load.htm*
- *www.softschools.com/language_arts/phonics/games/magic_e_sounds .jsp*
- *www.youtube.com/watch?v=NVeq9a4dFIU*
- *www.youtube.com/watch?v=7hTWuN0WCu4&feature=relmfu*

Decoding Two-Syllable Words

In 1st grade students should be able to decode two-syllable words by breaking them into their word parts. Recall the section of Reading: Foundational Skills standard 3 that reads:

Decode two-syllable words following basic patterns by breaking the words into syllables.

Single-Syllable Words	Two-Syllable Words
Cake	Believe
Run	Upset
Sun	Paper

To read two-syllable words, remind your child that each syllable has a vowel sound. To read the word she will have to break the word up between the syllables. Example: *believe* would be read be/lieve; *upset* would be read up/set. Practice reading two-syllable words with your child to reinforce this phonics skill.

Inflectional Endings

An inflectional ending refers to a suffix that is added to the base word to show verb tense, possession, comparison, or plurality. Recall the section of Reading: Foundational Skills standard 3 that reads:

Read words with inflectional endings.

Here is a list of words with inflectional endings to practice with your child:

- Bigger
- Taller
- Tallest
- Cleaner
- Cleanest
- Tom's
- Going
- Wanted

The key behind reading words with inflectional endings is to train kids to read to the end of the word. This can often be a struggle for kids. For example, they might read the word *bigger* as *big*, stopping at the one-syllable word that they know (big) and not look beyond it. Model for your child the importance of looking at the whole word and reading it until the end.

Literature

There are ten Reading: Literature standards in grade 1. The standards focus on reading closely to comprehend texts. Students in 1st grade will have the opportunity to develop a clear understanding of text features and different strategies to understand main ideas and topics. Here are some key factors to focus on with your child in reference to the reading literature standards.

Retell

The ability to retell the key ideas in a text that is read or listened to is a pertinent skill for 1st graders. Read the following text to your child and ask him or her to retell the story:

One day Gretchen and George went to visit their Aunt Francis in Texas. Aunt Francis was known for her baking. Gretchen could not wait to taste all the delicious treats that her aunt would make. Her favorites were the pralines and pecan pie. Yum, she could almost taste them now. George was not as excited. He was going to miss hanging out with his buddies. They had all made the baseball team next year, and while he was away in Texas his friends would be practicing at the park. When they finally arrived at Aunt Francis's house they were met with the smells of her wonderful baking. Gretchen and George both heard their stomachs grumble in anticipation of these delicious treats. George knew he would miss his friends, but after seeing Aunt Francis he was so happy he had come. She was his favorite aunt and he couldn't wait to spend time with her.

Ask the following questions to prompt your child with the retelling:

1. What was the story about? Tell me in your own words.
2. Was George excited about the visit? Use evidence from the story to support this idea.
3. What did Gretchen look forward to most?
4. How did George change by the end of the story?

You can repeat this activity with any story that you and your child read. The idea is to ask your child to go back into the text to support any conclusions she draws. Make sure your child backs up any claims with information that she read in the story.

Final Thoughts on the Reading: Literature Standards

Of these ten Reading: Literature standards, there are nine standards with multiple sub-standards. They focus on finding key details in a text, word meanings, comparing and contrasting information found in different texts, character analysis, and reading texts at grade level.

A few of these standards are highlighted here, as they are essential for your child to practice at home.

Being able to determine when the narrator shifts in a text is another important skill. Reading: Literature standard 6 reads:

Identify who is telling the story at various points in a text. Asking your child if the narrator of the story has changed when reading a text will help her begin to listen more carefully, which will increase her comprehension levels. Another way to reinforce this standard is to have your child read stories about the same topic from different points of view.

Some great books to consider are *The True Story of the Three Little Pigs!* by A. Wolf and, of course, the original "The Three Little Pigs" story. Book pairings like this allow kids to think about different perspectives. Practice at this sort of reading helps children more readily notice narrator shifts in other storybooks they read.

Vivid Details

Reading: Literature standard 7 reads:

Use illustrations and details in a story to describe its characters, setting, or events.

Your child should continually think about how details, including those in illustrations, help to enhance a story and make it more enjoyable for the reader. You want your child to start noticing these literary elements so that she starts including them in her own writing. Student writing should begin to have more vivid details in their drawings, and their sentences should start to become more detailed. Students should go beyond just telling the color of an apple, for example, and should be able to talk about how an apple smells and looks and sounds. Continue to highlight details with your child when you encounter them in books and illustrations.

Informational Text

As in kindergarten, Common Core standards require a 50/50 split between reading fictional and informational text in the 1st grade. There are ten Reading: Informational Text standards in 1st grade. These standards focus on identifying key ideas and details, text features, comparison, and reading fluency. The ability to comprehend factual information is increasingly important as students move through the grade-level bands.

Details

Reading: Informational Text standard 1 is exactly the same as Reading: Literature standard 1. It reads:

Ask and answer questions about key details in a text.

The key idea to remember is that comprehending text is the main focus in both fiction and informational text. Students should be able to identify the key ideas and details, and articulate them when asked.

Key details that students will look for in nonfiction, or informational text, include identifying the most important information about the topic and articulating a general summary of the text. Reiterate the importance of summarizing to your child, which will reinforce remembering key details.

Text Features

Understanding how nonfiction text is organized is an important skill to reinforce with your 1st grader. Reading: Informational Text standard 5 reads:

Know and use various text features (e.g., headings, tables of contents, glossaries, electronic menus, icons) to locate key facts or information in a text.

Be sure to share glossaries, icons on maps, tables of contents, and so on with your child as your encounter them. It will be important that your child understand how to read these text features for information. This will help your child comprehend the informational text and draw information to share.

FACT

Your child will encounter numerous informational texts over the course of his studies. Understanding how to use a glossary to obtain further information on a subject, or knowing how to read a key on a map, will set your child apart in his ability to maneuver and comprehend informational text.

Reading Multiple Texts

Continue to expose your child to multiple texts on subjects of interest. This was discussed in the kindergarten chapters, but it remains important throughout the grade levels. Reading: Informational Text standard 9 reads:

Identify basic similarities in and differences between two texts on the same topic (e.g., in illustrations, descriptions, or procedures).

Your child should be able to read numerous books and watch videos on topics of interest, and then be able to discuss the similarities and differences in the information provided. First graders should be able to independently discuss the similarities. You may have to prompt your child a little when it comes to talking about the differences.

Some topics your 1st grader may find interesting to review include:

- Extreme weather
- Holidays around the world
- Animals in the rainforest
- Sports teams

Reading Texts

The final standard this chapter discusses is Reading: Informational Text standard 10, which reads:

With prompting and support, read informational texts appropriately complex for grade 1.

Your child will be expected to read informational texts at the 1st-grade-level band with prompting and support. Practice reading these texts at home with your child. Ask comprehension questions and reinforce using the glossary to find out unknown words. Also model using the graphs and illustrations to help make the meaning clear. Most importantly, have your child summarize what she learns from her reading.

CHAPTER 12

Expectations in 1st Grade Writing

Reading and writing are connected skills, and as students move through the grade levels this becomes more evident by the tasks that they will be required to complete. There are seven writing standards for 1st graders. These standards focus on opinion pieces, informative pieces, and narratives. In 1st grade, students begin to focus on the audience, such that their writing speaks to the specific audience. Students in 1st grade should begin to understand the importance of peer editing and should begin to independently go back and check their own writing. Students should also be able to look for research materials to enhance their writing pieces. This chapter discusses key 1st grade writing standards and how you can support them at home.

Text Types and Purposes

Writing about oneself is something that students in 1st grade enjoy. Like kindergartners they have a keen sense of self and enjoy expressing their likes and wants. Storytelling is a natural part of growing up. Children are drawn to the wonder and magic of a well-told story.

ESSENTIAL

Writing is an important literacy skill that the 1st grade students must acquire. Please note that the Common Core ELA writing standards are meant to be taught in conjunction with the reading standards. Therefore, you may notice some connections between the expectations in reading and the expectations in writing.

One of the key writing genres in 1st grade is the narrative. First graders are expected to recount two or more appropriately sequenced events. For example, a narrative is a story in which your child writes about going shopping and returning home to cook with the ingredients purchased. Writing standard 3 reads:

Write narratives in which they recount two or more appropriately sequenced events, include some details regarding what happened, use temporal words to signal event order, and provide some sense of closure.

Appropriate sequencing is important when writing narratives. The standards require that students appropriately sequence two or more events. This requires that students ensure they are writing about events in the order in which they took place.

You can allow your child to create a timeline to capture the events he is going to write about. This will help your child recount the events in sequence. Practice sequencing events by having your child write about his day. Have him start with the morning and tell everything important that happened until bedtime. You can also have him write about his day at school. Have him write about the key details of the day, starting from when the bell rang to start the day until it rang to end the day.

You may notice that your child struggles with this task. He may want to include details about everything that happened in the day. Remind him to only share the key details of the day.

FACT

Developing writers do well when provided models for writing. Make writing fun for your child by asking questions about his piece.

Temporal Words

This standard also calls for students to use temporal words. Temporal words are prepositions used to show the position of an event. Here are some common temporal words for 1st graders:

on	by	to
after	until	while
within	except	during
between	following	for

ACTIVITY:

- Have your child use temporal prepositions in sentences.

PROCEDURE:

1. Model for your child how to use a temporal preposition in a sentence.
2. Write the following sentence: We went to the store after school.
3. Explain to your child that the word *after* represents when you went to the store.
4. Ask your child to write a sentence using the word *after*.
5. Have your child share the sentence.
6. Provide feedback on the sentence.

Another activity to try is to have your child locate temporal words in a story that you are reading. Read the story ahead to find temporal words. Continually encourage your child to include these words in his writing.

Closure

Writing standards 1–3 ask students to provide closure for their writing. Closure refers to signal words to end a writing piece. Many students end their writing pieces without including any type of closing statement. Closure can be a difficult concept for a 1st grader to internalize. For 1st grade students the best way to emphasize closure is to point it out when you are reading.

PROCEDURE:

1. Share the following with your child:

   John and Jack spent the day together at the park. They started the day playing on the monkey bars. They then went to play basketball with a few friends. They ended their fun day at the park by playing catch. The boys had a great day together, and plan to spend next Saturday at the park again.

2. Ask your child to tell you what the story was about.
3. Read the last sentence aloud.
4. Tell your child this is a conclusion.
5. Tell your child that his writing should always have a conclusion.
6. Ask your child to write a new conclusion to the story.
7. Help your child construct a conclusion sentence.
8. Reread the story with the new conclusion that you and your child wrote.

Having a strong closing or concluding sentence is an important writing feature your 1st grader should be using consistently. Have him move away from cliché closings like "And they lived happily ever after" and the oh, so boring "The End." By 1st grade your child should start experimenting with using different closure types.

Closure and Different Writing Types

Your child will be writing opinion pieces and informative/explanatory pieces. It is important to note that writing a closure for a narrative piece will differ from writing a closure for an informational piece. Writing standard 1 reads:

> Write opinion pieces in which they introduce the topic or name of the book they are writing about, state an opinion, supply a reason for the opinion, and provide some sense of closure.

Remember that opinion pieces can be persuasive in nature. This would be writing that requires your child to state her opinion regarding a 1st grade topic. She will need to provide all the necessary supporting details and also include an appropriate conclusion.

First graders can begin to restate their stand in their conclusion paragraph. This could look like the following:

> *As I noted in my paper, I believe that year-round school is a good idea. It will allow us to learn more and have more breaks throughout the school year.*

In this example, the child restated her opinion in the closing. Writing standard 2 reads:

> Write informative/explanatory texts in which they name a topic, supply some facts about the topic, and provide some sense of closure.

Collect some samples of opinion pieces and explanatory writing and go over the same procedure as previously mentioned to share different closures to the different genres. This will help your child become aware of the appropriate models for closure in different genre types. Remind your child to always proofread her drafts to ensure she has written a proper closing sentence.

Production and Distribution of Writing

Working with adults and peers to improve writing by editing and revising is a skill that develops across the grade levels. For grade 1, writing standard 5 reads:

With guidance and support from adults, focus on a topic, respond to questions and suggestions from peers, and add details to strengthen writing as needed.

ALERT

Some kids struggle with feedback. Ensure praise is provided to combat feelings of failure.

The key to this standard is that adult support is necessary for the skill to develop. It takes skill and precision to understand how to critique another student's work. To help your child grow in his ability to listen to feedback it will be important for you to read your child's writing and provide constructive feedback.

A tool to use is a constructive feedback form. An example of one follows. This tool will help you guide your child in the process of revision:

CONSTRUCTIVE FEEDBACK FORM
❑ Did you use chronological order in your writing?
❑ Did you explain important ideas?
❑ Did you remember to check for capitals, spacing, and punctuation?
❑ Can you add words to make your writing clearer for the reader?
❑ Did you include a concluding sentence?

Use these as a starting point to get your child thinking about his writing and the key elements in a good writing piece. The main thing to remember is to always stay positive with your comments and actions, and help your child make the necessary revisions to enhance his writing piece.

Digital Tools

Teaching kids keyboarding skills at an early age is becoming the norm. Here are some useful tools you can use to help your child develop keyboarding skills in a fun and play-like manner:

- *www.onlytypinggames.com/games/air-typer*
- *www.squiglysplayhouse.com/Games/MiniClip/Alphattack/index.php*
- *http://freeonlinetypinggames.com/kids-typing/alpha-dro*
- *http://freeonlinetypinggames.com/free-typing-games/finger-frenzy*
- *www.abcya.com/keyboarding_practice.htm*
- *www.learninggamesforkids.com/keyboarding_games/paragraph-writing-practice.html*

These online typing games make practicing keyboarding skills fun for children. Writing standard 6 reads:

With guidance and support from adults, use a variety of digital tools to produce and publish writing, including in collaboration with peers.

The standard also discusses working with peers and adults to produce writing. Again, the Common Core ELA standards push students toward working in collaborative groups to complete writing tasks. Continuing to encourage teamwork with your child is important.

Research Writing

One of the biggest shifts in 1st grade is the expectation for students to conduct research and write about it. Research writing is a big part of college and career readiness, thus starting to build on this skill in grade 1 is important. Writing standard 7 reads:

Participate in shared research and writing projects (e.g., explore a number of "how-to" books on a given topic and use them to write a sequence of instructions).

Having your child read a series of how-to books and having her write instructions is a great way to model how research is conducted and what goes into presenting those research findings. Here is a great way to help your child with this standard:

PROCEDURE:

1. Select 2 or 3 how-to texts.
2. Read the texts with your child.
3. As you read, write down key steps that are needed to complete the task.
4. After you have read all the books and written all your notes go over them together.
5. Create a new list with the steps in an order that makes sense to you and your child.
6. Create a new list of how-to steps with pictures.
7. Have your child share the how-to list with another family member.

Other shared research writing projects could include researching a pet. For example, if your family is considering adopting a new pet, you could have your child conduct research on different cat or dog breeds and have her share them with the rest of the family. This process could also be used to research a new car, bike, video game console, and so on.

Teaching kids the importance of conducting research to make decisions is a good way to reinforce and build research skills.

Gathering Research

You can do more to help your child conduct and write research texts. Standard 8 reads:

> With guidance and support from adults, recall information from experiences or gather information from provided sources to answer a question.

This standard teaches students to answer research questions. It starts to move kids toward the scientific method. The scientific method starts with a research question and moves on to developing a hypothesis, conducting an experiment, completing observations, and coming to a conclusion. You may find that your child's teacher uses this standard when conducting science experiments. It can also be used to answer questions in other content areas. The main intent of this standard is to answer a given question by conducting research or recalling information.

To help your child with this standard, have her complete mini science projects at home. Require your child to write about her findings. Here are some awesome websites that you can use that provide science experiments to conduct at home:

- *www.sciencebuddies.org/science-fair-projects/parent_resources.shtml*
- *www.sciencebob.com/experiments/index.php*

In summary, writing success in the 1st grade will require that your child apply the same skills she is using in her reading and writing standards. Having a keen understanding of the key ideas of these standards, and understanding how to write in multiple genres, will help you instruct your child. Encourage your child to read different genre styles and have her write using these styles. Keeping a journal (either a paper journal or an online journal) is a good way to encourage narrative writing. Support keyboarding by having your child practice writing using the computer. Finally, pay attention to informational texts. Point out the graphics, illustrations, and glossaries and discuss how they help the reader understand the information.

CHAPTER 13

Expectations in 1st Grade Speaking, Listening, and Language

The ability to express ideas orally is a building block for literacy development. Literacy includes the ability to speak in front of audiences for different purposes. First graders must continue to learn the rules of public speaking, including taking turns and using active listening strategies that were introduced in kindergarten. By the end of 1st grade, students should have mastered all of the preliminary listening and speaking skills so that they are ready to take off in 2nd grade where the speaking and listening tasks will become more complex. There are six Speaking and Listening standards and five Language standards for 1st grade. This chapter discusses the standards that your 1st grader will encounter.

Collaborative Conversations

First grade students are expected to participate in collaborative conversations regarding 1st grade topics.

Rules for Discussions

The standard notes the importance of having agreed-upon rules for oral discussions. Speaking and Listening standard 1 reads:

Participate in collaborative conversations with diverse partners about grade 1 topics and texts with peers and adults in small and larger groups.
a. Follow agreed-upon rules for discussions (e.g., listening to others with care, speaking one at a time about the topics and texts under discussion).
b. Build on others' talk in conversations by responding to the comments of others through multiple exchanges.
c. Ask questions to clear up any confusion about the topics and texts under discussion.

Your child's teacher should have rules for oral conversations in the classroom. You can request a copy of them so you can use the same verbiage when working with your child at home. As with kindergarten students, students in 1st grade need specific models of what collaborative conversations look like and sound like. You can model this for your child when discussing topics.

FACT

Children who engage in conversations with their parents build vocabulary and comprehension skills.

PROCEDURE:

1. Talk with your child about what she learned in school.
2. Ask questions to clear up any confusion of points that need elaboration.

3. Build on her ideas by adding information that will help clarify meaning. For example, you can add that you remember a time when you went on a field trip to the zoo or had lunch with a friend, and so on.

Model this mode of conversation to help your child understand the unstated rules of collaborative conversations.

Questioning

The ability to ask questions that are relevant and associated with the topic at hand is something that needs to be taught to 1st graders. Going off on a tangent and talking about things other than the topic is commonplace in primary classrooms. This standard specifically notes that the questions should relate to the topic and/or texts that are under discussion.

As a reminder, part of standard 1 states:

Ask questions to clear up any confusion about the topics and texts under discussion.

One way to help model this is by using a questioning chart. The following questioning chart can serve as a starting point to help your child craft questions in order to clarify meaning.

- Who?
- What?
- When?
- Where?
- Why?
- How?

You can also model questioning anytime you are reading a text, watching a movie, or watching or listening to any media. The key point to remember is that you want your child to start listening for clarity and asking questions to answer unknown information. Do not allow your child to digress and talk about topics other than the text and topic that you are exploring. Your child's teacher will thank you for helping to instill this skill.

Relevant Details

Students in 1st grade (and beyond) sometimes struggle with determining what details are most relevant in a text. Speaking and Listening standard 2 reads:

Ask and answer questions about key details in a text read aloud or information presented orally or through other media.

This standard notes that information may be coming from media sources as well as texts and books. When there is so much information being provided from so many sources, it can sometimes be difficult, or even tricky, to determine which details are most significant to overall meaning.

A good way to help students understand this concept is to have them describe someone or something that is important to them. When students use relevant details to describe their favorite pet or movie they begin to internalize key and relevant details. Here is a quick and fun way to help your child with relevant details:

MATERIALS:

- Drawing paper
- Markers
- Writing utensils

PROCEDURE:

1. Ask your child to draw a picture of something special to him. Let him know it can be a person, place, or a thing.
2. Once he has drawn his picture, have him go in and label the illustration.
3. Tell him to label the details in the drawing. Guide your child as he is labeling, reminding him of the important details that should be labeled or drawn in.
4. Discuss the illustration and the labels. Ask your child why he labeled certain things.
5. Talk about how the things he labeled that were important or relevant to him. Explain how when he reads or listens to text it is important that he thinks about the relevant details because that will help him understand it.

Clarifying

Clarifying meaning is a key skill that the Common Core ELA Speaking and Listening standards support. Speaking and Listening standard 3 reads:

> Ask and answer questions about what a speaker says in order to gather additional information or clarify something that is not understood.

Knowing how to ask for clarification when a topic or detail is unclear is a skill that 1st graders are expected to master. The standard notes that children are expected to question a speaker to gather further information to clarify meanings.

You may be thinking, "How can you teach something so abstract to a 1st grader?" The key here is to model the desired skill so that children can internalize it. An easy way to teach clarification is by asking the five W and one H questions (who, what, when, where, why, and how) when you are watching a newscast or listening to a speaker.

ESSENTIAL

Here is a great free website that provides news stories that are kid friendly. You can watch the news story and ask questions about the information that was presented: *www.dogonews.com.*

PROCEDURE:

1. Preview a news video to watch with your child on a kid-friendly news website.
2. Tell your child to think about the five W and one H questions as she watches the news story.
3. Give your child a sheet of paper to take notes about the five W and one H questions as she watches the news story.
4. Watch the news clip.
5. Discuss the questions answered from the clip.
6. Share any questions that may need clarification after watching the video.

Continue to model questioning strategies with your child. Ask for clarification on topics that you read and study. The more you model this skill, the more likely your child will start to incorporate it into her own skill bank.

Character Analysis

Another important skill that the Common Core ELA focuses on is expressing feelings. Both the feelings of the reader and the characters in the story are important to explore when reading a text. Speaking and Listening standard 4 reads:

Describe people, places, things, and events with relevant details, expressing ideas and feelings clearly.

Often teachers will have booktalks with children. During these booktalks kids speak about what they learned about the characters, setting, and events. The focus during the booktalks is on giving the audience an insight into the characters and what motivates them. This concept of talking about books and providing key insights ties into literary analysis. It asks children to not only describe the key details but to talk about the ideas and feelings of the characters explicitly. This requires students to read closely and analytically.

ESSENTIAL

A nice way to support Speaking and Listening standard 4 is to read a story that may be funny or sad with your child, and then ask your child to explain how she felt after reading the story. There are many wonderful stories that talk about feelings. Two great books are *The Way I Feel* by Janan Cain and *Feelings* by Aliki. Both stories discuss feelings and provide great illustrations to support the ideas.

To take this standard to text, you can read *Charlotte's Web* by E.B. White with your child and talk about the feelings that Wilbur and Charlotte each felt. This classic children's story provides insights into fear, sacrifice, and joy. This book is a great read aloud for your 1st grader. It has rich themes and ties perfectly into the character analysis that this standard asks for.

Recalling Details

Helping children develop their long- and short-term memory is another skill that the Common Core ELA standards require. Students are asked to recall relevant details from texts, both read and heard. Holding on to this information can be taught by playing memory games. There are many games that children can play to strengthen memory.

FACT

Children age five through seven need support with memory. Here are some websites with memory games: *www.zoodles.com/free-online-kids-games/first-1st-grade_memory* and *www.softschools.com/games/memory_games.*

There are many fun activities you can play with your child to improve memory. For example, you can read a list of details to your child and have him repeat them. Start with a list of three things and build on it as your child becomes better with holding on to things in his memory bank.

Visual Presentations

Students should be comfortable with using visuals in their oral presentation to help clarify meaning. Speaking and Listening standard 5 reads:

Add drawings or other visual displays to descriptions when appropriate to clarify ideas, thoughts, and feelings.

This standard is highly relevant for college and career readiness. Students in college courses are routinely asked to make presentations using digital media programs. Once in the workplace they may be asked to present using these same technologies. In many jobs, teams present their findings and income statements, quarterly reports, and so on using digital technologies.

Your 1st grade child may be asked to make a presentation using a poster board, software like PowerPoint, or other digital presentation programs.

Practice using visual aids for school presentations will help prepare your child for these future experiences.

Sentence Types

The final Speaking and Listening standard is standard 6. Standard 6 reads:

Produce complete sentences when appropriate to task and situation.

Students in 1st grade should be familiar with varied sentence types and should be comfortable using them. The most familiar sentence types are: exclamatory sentences, declarative sentences, imperative sentences, and interrogative sentences. The following chart will help you understand the different sentence types:

Interrogative	A sentence that asks a question. (Are you coming to the party?)
Declarative	A sentence that makes a statement. (I am going to bed.)
Imperative	A sentence that issues a command. (Go to the front of the line.)
Exclamatory	A sentence that expresses strong feelings. (I do not like spiders!)

Your child should be familiar with specialized sentences like these examples. Helping your child speak in complete sentences at all times is important because it establishes a good foundation for public speaking.

Conventions of Standard English

The Language standards in 1st grade focus on building student knowledge in English usage. There are five language standards in 1st grade.
Standard 1 reads:

Demonstrate command of the conventions of standard English grammar and usage when writing or speaking.
a. Print all upper- and lowercase letters.
b. Use common, proper, and possessive nouns.

c. Use singular and plural nouns with matching verbs in basic sentences (e.g., He hops; We hop).

d. Use personal, possessive, and indefinite pronouns (e.g., I, me, my; they, them, their, anyone, everything).

e. Use verbs to convey a sense of past, present, and future (e.g., Yesterday I walked home; Today I walk home; Tomorrow I will walk home).

f. Use frequently occurring adjectives.

g. Use frequently occurring conjunctions (e.g., and, but, or, so, because).

h. Use determiners (e.g., articles, demonstratives).

i. Use frequently occurring prepositions (e.g., during, beyond, toward).

j. Produce and expand complete simple and compound declarative, interrogative, imperative, and exclamatory sentences in response to prompts.

Supporting the use of adjectives to improve description is a good skill to support at home. Remember that adjectives are words used to describe. Have your child write sentences that describe common objects. Ask your child to use adjectives that make the descriptions come more alive. For instance, your child may write, "The gray and white cat sat under the tree." Now ask her to add more adjectives and make this description more vivid. She could write, "The small gray and white cat sat timidly under the tree."

Here are some sample adjectives to use with your child:

- Big
- Best
- Black
- Blue
- Bright
- Busy
- Clever
- Cold
- Dry
- Fancy
- Fast
- Fine
- Good
- Long
- Many
- Hard
- Loud
- Proud
- Rich
- Silent
- Ugly
- Warm
- Wild

Handwriting

Encourage your child to continue working on her handwriting skills. The standards call for students to be able to print all uppercase and lowercase letters fluidly. Your 1st grader should have no problem with printing letters. You can purchase a notebook and have your child practice forming letters. Here are a few websites that can help with letter formation:

- *www.ictgames.com/sky_writing.html*
- *literactive.com/Download/live.asp?swf=story_files/letter_formation_US.swf*
- *www.itchysalphabet.com/game.php*

Phonetic Spelling

The Language standards also call for using phonetic spelling to figure out unknown words. Standard 2 reads:

Demonstrate command of the conventions of standard English capitalization, punctuation, and spelling when writing.
a. Capitalize dates and names of people.
b. Use end punctuation for sentences.
c. Use commas in dates and to separate single words in a series.
d. Use conventional spelling for words with common spelling patterns and for frequently occurring irregular words.
e. Spell untaught words phonetically, drawing on phonemic awareness and spelling conventions.

Help to support your child with his sound spelling skills by having him practice spelling unknown words. You can do this verbally or by having your child write these words. Spelling is an important skill that you want to encourage in your child. When students are confident in their ability to spell, their writing becomes more fluid and comprehensible.

Strategies to Read Unknown Words

Students in the 1st grade should have a toolkit of strategies that they can use to determine the meaning of unknown words. Language standard 4 reads:

Determine or clarify the meaning of unknown and multiple-meaning words and phrases based on grade 1 reading and content, choosing flexibly from an array of strategies.
a. Use sentence-level context as a clue to the meaning of a word or phrase.
b. Use frequently occurring affixes as a clue to the meaning of a word.
c. Identify frequently occurring root words (e.g., look) and their inflectional forms (e.g., looks, looked, looking).

This standard breaks down several skills your child should be familiar with to determine the meaning of unknown words. Continue to support your child in using context clues to figure out unknown words. This will involve looking at a word in the context of the other words in the sentence to determine what that unknown word means.

Another strategy is to use affixes to determine word meanings. Affixes are prefixes and suffixes that are added to a base word to create a new meaning. Chapter 7 covered the most common affixes. You can use the chart in Chapter 7 to help your child understand the meaning of the most common prefixes and suffixes.

Categorizing Language

Students in 1st grade should be able to categorize words. Standard 5 reads:

With guidance and support from adults, demonstrate understanding of word relationships and nuances in word meanings.
a. Sort words into categories (e.g., colors, clothing) to gain a sense of the concepts the categories represent.
b. Define words by category and by one or more key attributes (e.g., a duck is a bird that swims; a tiger is a large cat with stripes).
c. Identify real-life connections between words and their use (e.g., note places at home that are cozy).
d. Distinguish shades of meaning among verbs differing in manner (e.g., look, peek, glance, stare, glare, scowl) and adjectives differing in intensity (e.g., large, gigantic) by defining or choosing them or by acting out the meanings.

By being able to categorize words into colors, shapes, and so forth, students gain an understanding of word meanings. They can then use these words in their own writing and speaking.

ALERT

Pay attention to how your child reacts when she encounters an unknown word in text. Does she try to sound out the word or does she look to you for help? Encourage your child to use strategies taught in her class to help when approaching unknown words. You want your child to develop independence and not rely on you to provide unknown words. Remind your child to use her strategies like looking at the first letter, seeing if she knows any part of the word, and using pictures (if the text has pictures) to figure out the unknown word.

The standard also encourages students to increase their vocabulary; understanding that there are multiple words with similar meanings could help increase it. Practice this skill at home by asking your child to find other ways to say words like *pretty* or *happy*. This is a wonderful way to build your child's vocabulary-making skills.

New Words

The final Language standard for 1st grade is standard 6. Standard 6 reads:

> Use words and phrases acquired through conversations, reading (and being read to), and responding to texts, including using frequently occurring conjunctions to signal simple relationships (e.g., because).

This standard encourages students to build their vocabulary by using new words and phrases they encounter in reading and listening tasks. You should encourage your child to try new words that she hears in the stories that you read together. As you will recall, the Common Core ELA standards have increased the text complexity for students, thus your child will be exposed to a richer vocabulary. Encourage your child to try at least one new word per day. This activity will help your child increase her vocabulary. This is important because research has found that improvements in vocabulary help students increase their grades in school.

Support Activities

DIRECTIONS: HAVE YOUR CHILD READ THE FOLLOWING STORY. SUPPORT YOUR CHILD WITH UNKNOWN WORDS AS NEEDED.

Once there were two bunnies. One was named Hop and the other was named Pop. The bunnies loved to munch on grass and carrots. They liked playing at the pond and watching the fish swim. Hop and Pop did everything together. They were like brothers.

1. Who are the characters in the story?
2. What is the setting of the story?
3. What is the main idea of the story? Give details from the text in your answer.

DIRECTIONS: HAVE YOUR CHILD USE THE WORD BANK AND WRITE THE SILENT E WORD THAT BEST COMPLETES EACH SENTENCE.

Word Bank
line bake nine cake plane

1. We like to _____ cookies.
2. He will be _____ years old on his next birthday.
3. The _____ at the movies was very long.
4. Have you ever flown in a _____?
5. I want a small piece of _____.

DIRECTIONS: HAVE YOUR CHILD UNDERLINE THE STATEMENTS.

1. I never eat breakfast.
2. Are you my friend?

3. We are going to the park.
4. You are a good friend.
5. I did not see the new car.

DIRECTIONS: HAVE YOUR CHILD PICK THE CORRECT PRONOUN THAT BELONGS IN THE SENTENCE.

1. _____ want to learn how to ride a bike. (I, me)
2. He and _____ like to play in the park. (me, I)
3. My dad showed _____ how to play baseball. (me, I)
4. _____ is my best friend. (she, me)
5. Jill and _____ are in the same class. (I, me)

DIRECTIONS: HAVE YOUR CHILD WRITE THE LETTERS OF THE ALPHABET, BOTH THE UPPER- AND LOWERCASE LETTERS.

DIRECTIONS: HAVE YOUR CHILD WRITE DIRECTIONS FOR A FRIEND ON HOW TO PLAY HER FAVORITE GAME.

CHAPTER 14

What Is Expected of Your 2nd Grade Student?

Students should enter 2nd grade as fluent readers who are able to comprehend and discuss key ideas in a text. The reading tasks in 2nd grade are more sophisticated as the texts become more complex and have deeper meaning. Students at this age level are able to process information more readily than before and have a keener sense of story and the elements of story. They can have deeper-level conversations about key ideas and can help expand on topics. This chapter discusses the Common Core Reading standards in 2nd grade.

Expectations in Reading

The reading expectations in the Common Core increase when students enter 2nd grade. Second graders begin to read to comprehend and they are charged with understanding the fine nuances in words. For example, they are asked to understand the meanings of colloquial phrases and figures of speech. Second graders are bridging the gap from basic decoding and are called to read with fluency and accuracy.

FACT

According to DIBELS, the Dynamic Indicators of Basic Early Literacy Skills, 2nd grade students should end the year reading 100 words per minute.

The key is to continue to have your child read, read, read. There is no way to learn to enjoy reading and develop fluency other than by reading. There are so many wonderful and interesting texts that can help your child build his love of reading. By 2nd grade you should be exposing your child to small chapter books. These young readers should also be building their stamina so that they can read for extended periods of time for enjoyment and to acquire information.

The Common Core has increased the complexity of texts for all students. There is also an expectation for students to read complex vocabulary and use context clues and their knowledge of prefixes and suffixes to determine meaning. Exposing your child to complex texts with robust vocabulary will help prepare him to read complex words and determine their meaning. These skills were taught in kindergarten and 1st grade, and students are expected to have perfected them by 2nd grade.

Foundational Skills

There are two Reading: Foundational Skills standards for students in 2nd grade. They are Reading: Foundational Skills standards 3 and 4. As noted in the previous section, students in 2nd grade should be decoding and reading grade-level text fluently.

To help you understand these two very important reading foundation standards, let's take a closer look at each of them:

Phonics and Word Analysis

Reading: Foundational Skills standard 3 reads:

Know and apply grade-level phonics and word analysis skills in decoding words.

a. Distinguish long and short vowels when reading regularly spelled one-syllable words.

b. Know spelling-sound correspondences for additional common vowel teams.

c. Decode regularly spelled two-syllable words with long vowels.

d. Decode words with common prefixes and suffixes.

e. Identify words with inconsistent but common spelling-sound correspondences.

f. Recognize and read grade-appropriate irregularly spelled words.

Let's simplify the phonics skills that this standard addresses. The first skill is to read and spell words with long and short vowels.

Here is a list of long and short vowel words appropriate for grade 2:

SHORT VOWELS	LONG VOWELS
cat	see
sit	make
bed	cake
fox	bee
swap	size
cup	old
saw	toe
put	pay
her	day
cow	say
sad	lay

ALERT

Having a firm understanding of long and short vowels is necessary. As your child progresses in grade levels, she will be responsible for decoding multi-syllabic words. A chart with long and short vowels can be found in Appendix B of this book. Use this as a tool to review long and short vowels with your child.

Students can show their knowledge of long and short vowels by distinguishing long and short vowel single-syllable words in an activity called *word sort*.

WORD SORT

MATERIALS:

- Index cards with the words from the previous list written on them
- Two index cards (one labeled "short vowels" and one labeled "long vowels")

PROCEDURE:

1. Mix the cards up.
2. Have your child read each word and place it in the appropriate category: long or short vowels.

Vowel Teams

Vowel teams are groups of two, three, or four vowels that team up to make unique sounds. Examples of vowel teams include: *ea, oi, oo*. Students learned vowel teams like *oa, ee,* and *ai* by the end of 1st grade. In 2nd grade they will read and spell words with the vowel teams *aw, au, ie, igh, oo, oi, oy,* and *ue*.

To reinforce vowel teams have your child practice writing words with common vowel teams. To make it fun you can use colored chalk or smelly markers to write the words.

Example:

au	ay	ai
Paul	hay	mail
haul	may	pail

Fluency

Reading texts fluently is another aim of the 2nd grade foundation standards. Reading: Foundational Skills standard 4 reads:

Read with sufficient accuracy and fluency to support comprehension.
a. Read on-level text with purpose and understanding.
b. Read on-level text orally with accuracy, appropriate rate, and expression on successive readings.
c. Use context to confirm or self-correct word recognition and understanding, rereading as necessary.

By the 2nd grade, your child should be reading 100 words per minute fluently. Reading fluency has long been associated with reading comprehension. Allow your child to read texts aloud as a means of practicing his oral reading skills. You can also try Readers Theater plays to help practice fluency.

ESSENTIAL

Have your family members practice reading scripts to model fluent reading. It is a fun way to reinforce fluency. Here are some websites with Readers Theater scripts: *www.teachingheart.net/readerstheater.htm*, and *www.thebestclass.org/rtscripts.html*.

To encourage fluent reading for your 2nd grader, have him practice reading phrases. Ensure that he is able to read these common phrases fluently:

- In the beginning
- Once upon a time
- He said
- She said
- You and I
- The people
- I see the
- When we go
- After a while
- Here we go
- What did you see

These are just a few fluency phrases you can have your child read. Add others to the list and have your child practice them. Remember to choose phrases that you encounter a lot in the texts that you read. These can be common phrases used in storybook and nonfiction texts.

Rereading

Students in 2nd grade must be comfortable rereading selections and sections of text to build their understanding of them. How many times have you had to reread a text to gain clarity? Model this practice with your child. As you read with your child, purposely pause to reread sections to clarify meaning. This is going to be especially important as your child is exposed to more complex texts in school.

Literature

The Reading: Literature standards continue to build on students' ability to ask questions, infer meanings, and determine key ideas and details in texts. Students will begin to apply more analysis as they explore an author's purpose for writing a text. This knowledge should be indicated in the students' writing and speaking and listening tasks.

Demonstrate Understanding

Reading: Literature standard 1 reads:

Ask and answer such questions as who, what, where, when, why, and how to demonstrate understanding of key details in a text.

This standard is present in not only kindergarten and 1st grade, but it continues in the 2nd grade and through all the grade levels. The skill of asking clarifying questions to make meaning is something that you want to continue modeling for your child.

Fables and Folktales and Diversity

One of the core goals of the Common Core ELA standards is to include more diversity in student learning. This is to prepare students to live in a more diverse and global society. Reading: Literature standard 2 reads:

> Recount stories, including fables and folktales from diverse cultures, and determine their central message, lesson, or moral.

This standard is very interesting because it specifically calls for students to read fables and folktales from different cultures. This standard also reminds teachers to bring a diversity of fiction to their classrooms so that students can have exposure to them.

One of the key things that students will need to learn is the structure of fables and folktales. This standard can be reinforced at home by reading fables and folktales to your child. As you read, talk to your child about the setting, characters, and the meaning or moral of the story.

Likewise, determining the moral of a story is an important skill that 2nd grade students need to master. For children at this age, mastery comes from practicing the skills that you model for them.

Character Analysis

Examining the actions of characters to determine why they behave in certain ways is another skill that 2nd grade students must master. Reading: Literature standard 3 reads:

> Describe how characters in a story respond to major events and challenges.

Analyzing characters and determining what motivates them continues to be an important standard that the authors of the Common Core ELA standards stress. When reading, your child will need to think about how the characters are reacting in relation to one another and in relation to what is happening in the story. This skill will be important as students progress through the grades and encounter increasingly complex texts that have complicated themes and ideas. Encourage your child to think about how characters respond in the stories that you read together.

Poetry

Poetry is a genre that children usually enjoy reading. In poetry, the word choice of a piece and its structural development are very well planned out.

Students will begin to learn about these concepts in 2nd grade. Reading: Literature standard 4 reads:

> Describe how words and phrases (e.g., regular beats, alliteration, rhymes, repeated lines) supply rhythm and meaning in a story, poem, or song.

Your child should be reading poetry in class and having discussions about rhyme and repeated lines. To help support this standard at home, read poetry with your child and ask him what he thinks about the rhyme scheme, alliteration, and repeated lines. Don't look for right or wrong answers. Rather, use this is an opportunity to see how your child views the poems and the feelings they evoke in him.

Here are some important poetry terms to keep in mind as you have your discussions.

Rhyme Scheme	The pattern in which the lines of a poem rhyme. (In this example, the (a) lines rhyme and the (b) lines rhyme.)
	Example:
	I am happy to be (a)
	Sitting here with thee (a)
	I know you are away (b)
	So please don't make me stay (b)
Alliteration	The use of the same repeated consonant sound.
	Example:
	Sam the silly snake
	Sat on a sandy stake
	So silly Sally had to stay
Repeated Lines	Also called a couplet or refrain. When lines are repeated for emphasis in a poem.
	Example:
	He that is brave
	Has no worry or pain
	He that is brave
	Knows how to behave
	He that is brave
	In this example, "He that is brave" is repeated to emphasize the theme of bravery.

Story Structure

Second graders should be proficient in describing the structure of a story by analyzing how the plot unfolds. Standard 5 reads:

Describe the overall structure of a story, including describing how the beginning introduces the story and the ending concludes the action.

This standard has to do with students following the plot of a story from beginning to end. This requires students to have a firm understanding of how stories develop.

Here is a simple story plot map that you can use with your child:

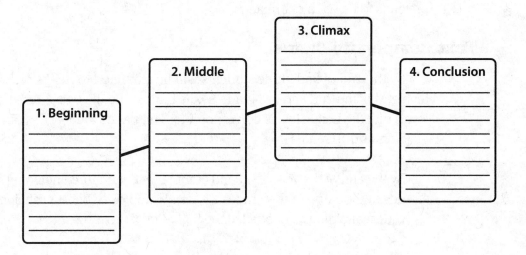

Dialogue

If you ever have the chance to watch a group of elementary students rehearsing for a play, you'll see how much they get into changing their voices for the different characters. Reading: Literature standard 6 hits on this. Standard 6 reads:

Acknowledge differences in the points of view of characters, including by speaking in a different voice for each character when reading dialogue aloud.

Children should be able to detect mood and tone by internalizing what a character may sound like if she were speaking aloud. For example, a wicked witch would sound very different from a fairy princess.

Have your child practice voices for the following characters:

- A tired old man
- A very happy child
- A hungry wolf
- A small mouse
- An angry lion

Talk to your child about how her voice and word choice change as she pretends to be each character.

Text Complexity Bands

By the end of 2nd grade students will be expected to read stories on the high end of the 2nd and 3rd grade Lexile bands. (Lexile bands are the grade levels that the Lexile levels correspond to. The bands are K–1, 2–3 and 4–5.) Standard 10 reads:

By the end of the year, read and comprehend literature, including stories and poetry, in the grades 2–3 text complexity band proficiently, with scaffolding as needed at the high end of the range.

Allow your child to read and listen to fictional stories that are at the higher levels on the Lexile band. Discuss the words that are confusing and talk about the theme of each story. This will help your child gain an appreciation for texts that are complex as she uses her comprehension strategies to figure out meaning.

Informational Text

Understanding how to ask questions to clarify meaning is important when reading informational text. Students in 2nd grade should be comfortable asking questions to better understand the context of the texts they are reading. They should also be familiar with identifying main ideas and topics in multiple paragraphs. These standards fall under Reading: Informational Text standards 1 and 2.

Demonstrate Understanding and Identify the Main Topic

Standard 1 reads:

Ask and answer such questions as who, what, where, when, why, and how to demonstrate understanding of key details in a text.

Standard 2 reads:

Identify the main topic of a multiparagraph text as well as the focus of specific paragraphs within the text.

When reading informational texts with your child—texts like articles, brochures, and manuals—be sure to discuss the main ideas or topics in each paragraph as you are reading. Informational text breaks up important details into sections. Your child needs to understand how this text structure works so she can become proficient in distinguishing individual sections and locating key ideas within each.

One way to have your child practice this skill is to have her create her own informational pamphlet. The pamphlet should include different sections, each with pertinent information, and can contain photos or pictures as well as text.

Finding Connections

Reading: Informational Text standard 3 reads:

Describe the connection between a series of historical events, scientific ideas or concepts, or steps in technical procedures in a text.

Reading about a series of historical events or scientific ideas helps children see how one event may influence subsequent events in a chain reaction of cause and effect. For instance, the attack on the World Trade Center towers on September 11, 2001, was the cause of America going to war. You can support this standard by talking with your child about the connections between a series of historical events and scientific ideas.

Here are some other ideas to consider discussing:

- Rain cycle
- Civil rights movement
- Elections

Text features

When reading nonfiction texts, it's important that students be able to effectively use text-based features to help clarify meaning. This skill is emphasized in Reading: Informational Text standard 5. Standard 5 reads:

Know and use various text features (e.g., captions, bold print, sub-headings, glossaries, indexes, electronic menus, icons) to locate key facts or information in a text efficiently.

In such works, captions, subheadings, and indexes all serve the purpose of helping to clarify meaning. Have your child identify the different text features in an informational text. Ask him to explain what each text feature is and identify its purpose. For example:

Captions help . . .	
Bold print is used to . . .	
Subheadings help . . .	
The glossary . . .	
An index . . .	
Electronic menus are used to . . .	
Icons help . . .	

Identifying Evidence

When reading informational text, your child should be able to identify the examples an author uses to support a position on a topic. This will require closely reading the text and assessing the evidence the author uses to make the claim. This is covered in Reading: Informational Text standard 8. Standard 8 reads:

Describe how reasons support specific points the author makes in a text.

Discuss the texts that you read with your child and talk about the ideas the author shares to support his or her ideas. You can practice this when you read stories aloud or work with your child on the readings she uses in class. Good books to use for this standard are informational texts that present facts about common issues like global warming or the need to recycle.

Compare and Contrast

Your child should also be able to compare the claims used in two different texts on the same subject. This will require finding the claims or evidence in each respective article or text and comparing them. This is described in standard 9. Standard 9 reads:

Compare and contrast the most important points presented by two texts on the same topic.

Comparison is an important skill set that college and career ready individuals possess. It requires analyzing how the arguments are alike and how they differ.

You can use a Venn diagram to help your child understand the logic behind comparing and contrasting. Venn diagrams are often used to represent commonalities and differences between different sets of things. In reading, Venn diagrams are often used to describe the similarities and differences between characters. Venn diagrams use overlapping circles to note the similarities on one side and the differences on the other side. The area where the circles overlap is used to write the things that are the same about the two objects being compared.

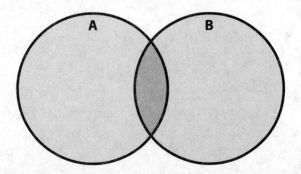

Technical Text Bands

The ability to read and comprehend nonfiction technical, scientific, and social studies texts is the goal of Reading: Informational Text standard 10. Standard 10 reads:

By the end of the year, read and comprehend informational texts, including history/social studies, science, and technical texts, in the grades 2–3 text complexity band proficiently, with scaffolding as needed at the high end of the range.

As you can see, the standard requires that students read texts at the 2nd and 3rd grade level proficiently. To achieve this standard your 2nd grader will need to be reading texts at the high end of the text complexity band independently, with support and scaffolding as necessary. This means that your child will be reading challenging texts and will need to struggle with them productively to make meaning. Your child will need to be comfortable using context clues, illustrations, graphs, and glossaries to help make meaning. To support this at home, continue to encourage your child to read texts that are a stretch for her. This will help her to become comfortable with the constructive struggle and inspire her to keep at it.

CHAPTER 15

Expectations in 2nd Grade Writing

Students in 2nd grade are capable of creating longer pieces of writing. As in the previous grade levels they are expected to write narratives, opinions, and informative pieces. Second graders are expected to have moved beyond inventive spelling or using phonetic sounds to spell unfamiliar words, and should be using their knowledge of spelling patterns and vowel teams to spell words correctly. They should also be moving from writing simple sentences to compound sentences with details. You may notice that your child is required to create longer pieces of writing and go through the editing process by completing multiple revisions on a draft. Second grade writing is very exciting for students because they find that they are able to express themselves in more concrete and descriptive ways. This chapter will explore 2nd grade writing in terms of the Common Core.

Text Types and Purposes

As students grow in their writing skills the writing tasks they will be asked to complete in the Common Core will become more complex in nature. For example, 2nd graders are asked to provide adequate evidence to support their opinion pieces. Writing standard 1 reads:

> Write opinion pieces in which they introduce the topic or book they are writing about, state an opinion, supply reasons that support the opinion, use linking words (e.g., because, and, also) to connect opinion and reasons, and provide a concluding statement or section.

As you can see, the writing tasks are becoming more complex and require more steps. First grade students are asked to complete the same task, but the difference in 2nd grade is that teachers expect linking words to show connection between ideas. This requires students to investigate a topic in order to provide those connections. This standard also asks that students include a conclusion to wrap up their writing piece. Continue to remind your child of this so that he learns to end his writing pieces with an appropriate concluding sentence.

Adequate Evidence

For a student in 2nd grade adequate evidence to support opinions would include evidence from a text or texts that he has read. It could also include connections to other stories that he has read. This moves away from surface-level conclusions and requires students to find the most appropriate support to include in a writing piece.

Students will have been working on this standard of supporting their opinions in kindergarten and 1st grade, so by 2nd grade they should be comfortable with using text evidence in their writing.

Continue to encourage your child to provide evidence for his opinions. Simply ask the question, "why?" Why questions open the door for your child to expound on his opinions, which is a necessary component of opinion writing pieces.

Forming Opinions

In order to form opinions, students will need to have access to multiple sources of information on a given topic of study. Students are expected to read several books on a topic in order to formulate opinions. To support this at home, allow your child to read multiple books and conduct research online for information on a desired topic. Try to help your child find books that have different points of view to help him acquire different perspectives. This type of research will be important as students move through the grade bands. As a reminder, opinion writing in the Common Core must be founded on text-based evidence and cannot be supported by personal opinion. Here is some language you can use with your child to help him focus on the text when writing about his opinions on topics.

TEXT-BASED EVIDENCE LANGUAGE

1. What support from the text can you include?
2. What in the text helped you form this opinion?
3. How did the text help you come to this conclusion?
4. Where in the text did you find support for this idea?

ALERT

Students sometimes confuse text-based evidence with just repeating everything in the text. The evidence cited must correspond with the particular question asked and will require students to read the text and find the most specific and accurate evidence from the text.

Linking Words

Using linking words or transitions to connect ideas is a writing strategy that 2nd grade students should begin to use. Linking words are important to help the reader follow along with a writer's train of thought. Many students struggle with transition words. They are so busy trying to get all the facts and information down on the page that they often forget about the writing basics. It is important to encourage your child to use transitions, and it is a writing skill he must master in order to successfully progress through the grade levels.

Common linking words or transitions include: *first, next, finally, then,* and *because*. Your child should start incorporating these words into his writing. Here is an activity to help encourage using transitions in writing.

Common Linking Words	
And	After
Also	Although
Besides	Before
Contrary to	In addition to
While	If
However	Despite
Then	When
But	Nevertheless
So	Because
However	

Have your child practice using the correct transition word in the following sentences:

I had to go to bed early _____ it was past my bedtime.

Yesterday, we read a story about George Washington, _____ today we read one about Abraham Lincoln.

First, I woke up, _____ I brushed my teeth and went to school.

You can practice with sentences like these and build on them as your child improves his ability to use transitions in his speaking and writing.

ALERT

Students sometimes confuse transitions and throw them in without determining the best word choice. Be cautious of this.

Another activity is to have your child highlight transitions in stories that you read in the newspaper and in magazines. Make a game out of finding transitions in the texts that you read. The more you bring transitions to your child's attention, the more likely he will incorporate them into his own writing pieces.

Narrative Writing

Narrative pieces should have a strong sense of story and well-developed characters and events. The specifications for the narrative writing standards in 2nd grade are contained in Writing standard 3. Writing standard 3 reads:

> Write narratives in which they recount a well-elaborated event or short sequence of events, include details to describe actions, thoughts, and feelings, use temporal words to signal event order, and provide a sense of closure.

Let's look at the requirement for recounting well-elaborated events or sequences of events. In the 2nd grade this will involve providing well-detailed information about the events that students are writing about. This requires students to go beyond a simple description of going to the park or to the playground. A well-elaborated account might include specifics about what was happening at the park or playground. It might include details about what the weather was like, what the surroundings looked like, what was happening on the scene, and so on.

You can help your child include more elaborate descriptions in her narratives by using the following chart:

SETTING
- Where does your story take place?
- What does it look like?
- What does it feel like?
- What can you hear?
- What can you smell?

CHARACTERS

- Who are the characters in your story?
- What do they look like?
- What do they sound like?
- What dialogue can you add?
- How do they react to the other characters in the story?

EVENTS

- What is happening in your story?
- What are the most important events that you want your reader to understand?
- How does your story end?

Ask your child to put details in each of the categories. Explain that these details should help the reader see, hear, and feel what is happening in the story.

Explanatory Writing

As with narrative writing, 2nd grade informative/explanatory writing should have more concrete details and finesse. Writing standard 2 addresses this topic. Writing standard 2 reads:

Write informative/explanatory texts in which they introduce a topic, use facts and definitions to develop points, and provide a concluding statement or section.

As the standard states, introducing a topic is an important skill that your 2nd grader will want to master. This means your child must learn how to introduce a writing piece in an appropriate manner and not just jump into a subject. This can be a challenge for students. They often just want to start rambling off facts and figures without properly introducing the topic.

Here are some simple starters for your child's informative/explanatory writing tasks.

How to Start an Informative/Explanatory Writing Piece

START WITH AN INTERESTING STATISTIC OR FACT.

- Example: There are more than 400 species of sharks in the world.

START BY ASKING A QUESTION.

- Did you know that the average person watches more than thirty-four hours of television each week?

START WITH A QUOTE.

- "Ask not what your country can do for you, ask what you can do for your country."
These famous words tell us the importance of helping others.

START BY DEFINING TERMS THAT ARE INTERESTING.

- According to the Merriam-Webster dictionary, the definition of citizen-ship is "the fact or status of being a citizen of a particular place."

These are just some simple suggestions for writing captivating introductions. Have your child look at informative texts and note how other authors introduce their writing. This can serve as a catalyst for her own writing pieces.

Explaining Ideas

Writing explanatory texts to meet Common Core standards requires that 2nd graders share their found knowledge of topics to explain a process or event. Students will develop this skill by reading texts on a subject and by obtaining information using digital sources like Internet articles, videos, and so on. They will then be asked to present this information in written format. Writing standard 6 supports the requirements established in Writing standard 2. Standard 6 reads:

With guidance and support from adults, use a variety of digital tools to produce and publish writing, including in collaboration with peers.

Explanatory writing can be presented in the form of a report, brochure, or a pamphlet. You can help your child practice this skill by having her make reports or brochures that capture information about topics of interest. When creating the piece it will be very important for you to show your child the different text types and sections that are expected. For example:

REPORT
- Title
- Introduction
- Interesting fact
- Pictures and/or illustrations
- Conclusion

BROCHURE/PAMPHLET
- Outer cover with a title
- Important facts and information
- Illustrations and graphics to support the topic

Editing and Revising

You may find that your child is taking a longer time to complete writing tasks in 2nd grade than she was in earlier grades. This is probably because the teacher will be expecting your child to revise and edit her work to make it more comprehensible. Working with peers to collaborate on writing and editing tasks is an important social skill that is developed throughout the grade levels. Writing standard 5 notes that 2nd grade students must work with adults and peers to edit their writing and make it stronger. Writing standard 5 reads:

With guidance and support from adults and peers, focus on a topic and strengthen writing as needed by revising and editing.

Peer editing has been taught in the classroom for years, so this is nothing new. The major shift here is that the editing process is emphasized in the standards throughout the grade levels. This stresses the high importance of this skill set.

As a parent, providing feedback to your child as she writes is a great way to reinforce revision and editing skills. This will allow your child to remain comfortable with the task. Use the following rubric with your 2nd grade student.

2ND GRADE WRITING RUBRIC
- ❑   I included a title
- ❑   I introduced the topic
- ❑   I have at least 3 supporting details
- ❑   I used transitional words
- ❑   I have a strong conclusion
- ❑   I checked my writing for spelling errors
- ❑   I checked my writing for grammar errors (capitals, commas, ending punctuation)
- ❑   I read my writing aloud to make sure it sounds right

Spelling

Students in kindergarten and 1st grade often spell unknown words using phonetic spelling patterns. However, students in 2nd grade should be moving away from inventive spelling. By the 2nd grade, your child should be comfortable with spelling words with irregular lettering patterns. These include words like *aren't*, *weren't*, *ache*, *echo*, and *school*.

ALERT

Some children and adults are poor spellers. Encourage your child to use the dictionary and to read more to help increase his spelling skills. The more your child reads the better his spelling will become.

Here is a list of frequently misspelled words for 2nd graders:

about	everybody	our	upon
again	favorite	outside	very
a lot	first	people	want
and	friend	said	went
another	could	scared	what
baseball	sometimes	were	when
because	heard	that's	with
before	house	their	would
I	then	whole	
could	know	there	
didn't	little	they	
night	thought	too	
every	once	two	

Practice the words on this list with your child. Have her spell the words and use them in sentences. This will help her to gain a good understanding of the meaning of each word.

Reports

Research writing is very important in the Common Core standards. Students will be reading more nonfiction texts and writing more about those texts. Second graders will be expected to write research papers that reflect the course of study that they conduct. Writing standard 7 calls for group research, which means students will be working with their peers to conduct research and write research reports. Writing standard 7 reads:

> Participate in shared research and writing projects (e.g., read a number of books on a single topic to produce a report; record science observations).

This standard explicitly notes the expectation for students to work in peer groups to record science observations and create reports. This is where collaboration skills are important. Expect your child to have group writing assignments in the 2nd grade. Check on his progress with the group work.

Gathering Information

Students in 2nd grade will be responsible for answering research questions in writing. This will require that they gather or recall information to back up their claims. This is stressed in Writing standard 8. Writing standard 8 reads:

> Recall information from experiences or gather information from provided sources to answer a question.

Your child should be comfortable with conducting research to answer questions. This research may involve reading a section of a text or may require doing some outside research on the Internet. Encourage this practice at home by having your child research subjects of interest. If you are taking a family trip you can involve your child in doing some online research and writing a summary of those findings for the family. Again, this is a high-weighted skill in the Common Core because it will follow students throughout their college and career lives. Comfortably conducting this type of short research to verify facts is a much needed skill in today's workplace.

Building Independence in Writing

Writing in the 2nd grade is a very exciting adventure. Students are becoming more independent in their writing tasks. They should have a firm understanding of how to incorporate facts and information into informational writing tasks. They should also have no problem writing narrative texts with well-developed characters and settings. Continue to support your child's writing and encourage him to use it as an important mode of communication.

CHAPTER 16

Expectations in 2nd Grade Speaking, Listening, and Language

The Common Core standards for 2nd grade build on the speaking and listening standards in kindergarten and 1st grade. In those grade levels teachers did a lot of modeling and prompting to help students understand what appropriate tone and intonation are needed for group speaking tasks. By the time students enter 2nd grade they should be more familiar with public speaking and have an idea of how to present ideas in a group setting. These students will be asked to present information orally and respond to listening tasks in an effort to hone their public speaking skills. The standards covered in this chapter require activities like collaborative conversations, active listening, and summarizing.

Comprehension and Collaboration

Building upon another student's thinking to continue a conversation is a skill that students are responsible for in 2nd grade. Students will learn to build on the ideas of others by linking their own thoughts and ideas to agree or disagree with what their classmates say. This will require that students learn to use the appropriate tone when speaking with others and the rules of speaking in order.

Collaborative Conversations

These requirements are highlighted in Speaking and Listening standard 1. Speaking and Listening standard 1 reads:

Participate in collaborative conversations with diverse partners about grade 2 topics and texts with peers and adults in small and larger groups.
a. Follow agreed-upon rules for discussions (e.g., gaining the floor in respectful ways, listening to others with care, speaking one at a time about the topics and texts under discussion).
b. Build on others' talk in conversations by linking their comments to the remarks of others.
c. Ask for clarification and further explanation as needed about the topics and texts under discussion.

Because all the standards are connected in the Common Core, collaborative conversation is related to opinion-based writing in which students express their opinions using research in written formats. Understanding how to courteously express an opinion is a skill that is necessary on many occasions such as when debating in class, or when asking for clarification on an issue. Continue to model how to express opinions in a polite manner whenever possible.

Encourage Being Inquisitive

Asking for clarification is also highlighted in this standard. Students in 2nd grade need to be comfortable asking for clarification if they do not understand a concept or idea. This is a skill that has to be nurtured in students. Sometimes students do not feel comfortable asking for clarification.

Speaking and Listening standard 3 is designed to help children overcome this issue. Speaking and Listening standard 3 reads:

> Ask and answer questions about what a speaker says in order to clarify comprehension, gather additional information, or deepen understanding of a topic or issue.

FACT

Asking questions for clarification is a sign of intelligence. Unfortunately, many see it as a weakness.

Many students don't feel comfortable asking for clarification because they do not want to appear to be inept. This is a very important issue that you should address with your child. You can help your child become comfortable in asking for clarification by helping him improve his active listening skills.

Active Listening

Active listening involves listening to another person in order to understand the key ideas that she trying to communicate. Body language that indicates active listening includes facing the person who is speaking, giving the speaker eye contact, having total focus on what the speaker is saying, answering questions as appropriate, and asking appropriate questions.

ALERT

Active listening skills are important, as students will be required to listen to information and share the information orally, including key ideas and details. This requires a focused effort on the part of the child to listen closely and determine which details are most important.

Students will need to recall information heard in media or that was read aloud. This requires that the child actively listen and attend to the information that is provided. You can support this at home by having your child listen to books on tape or audio books online. After listening to the texts have your child tell you the key ideas and details from the story.

You can also practice this skill by having your child listen to a news story on the radio. After listening, ask your child what the news story was about and what the key ideas were. Be sure to set a purpose for the activity before you start. Let your child know that as he listens he should be sure to listen for the key ideas and details. You can use the following chart to help your child:

AS YOU LISTEN, THINK ABOUT THE FOLLOWING:

FOR NONFICTION STORIES OR NEWS STORIES:
- What are the main ideas?
- What does the speaker want me to learn about?
- What are the most important details I don't want to forget?

FOR FICTION:
- Who are the main characters?
- Where is the story set?
- What is the main event in the story?
- What happens at the end of the story?

Teaching your child to think about these questions as he reads or listens to text is a great way to improve his ability to listen actively. This work also reinforces comprehension skills.

Deeper Understandings

Students will begin to develop deeper understandings of topics in 2nd grade. Students will demonstrate this knowledge by clarifying meaning and gathering additional information to increase their knowledge base. To accomplish this, students must conduct research on topics of interest. You can help your child gain an interest in conducting research by encouraging her to go to the library and check out books on topics of interest.

Recording Stories

Students in 2nd grade are asked to record stories and poems. Speaking and Listening standard 5 reads:

> Create audio recordings of stories or poems; add drawings or other visual displays to stories or recounts of experiences when appropriate to clarify ideas, thoughts, and feelings.

There are many tools that students can use to create audio recordings of stories. Back in your school days your teacher might have used a cassette recorder to have you record your story or poem. Today, students can create podcasts on a computer to record their voices. Podcasts are digital media files that can be uploaded on the Internet. They are very popular because they provide users the ability to transfer music, voice, or other file types into a package that others can download and enjoy.

Podcasts are a great way to engage students with technology. Students love to create sound recordings that include music and pictures. They are also very easy to create. All you need is a microphone and mixing/recording software. A podcast can even be created using only a smartphone.

FACT

GarageBand is a software application that allows you to record music or create podcasts. You can play around with GarageBand to help your child with voice recordings.

Here is a list of websites that provide more information on clever ways to use the podcast tool with kids to create stories:

- *www.justonemorebook.com*
- *www.storynory.com*
- *www.jtwgroup.com*

After your child records his story have him listen to the recording and talk about what he likes about his story recording and what he can do to make it better or what he wants to fix. Have him practice and rerecord as necessary. This is an excellent activity to reinforce fluency because it allows your child to hear how his reading sounds so that he can adjust as necessary.

Having your child talk about his own recording will help him enhance his critiquing skills. Critiquing skills are very important, because they cross so many areas. He will apply this skill to his peer evaluations in speaking and listening and in writing. Helping your child develop an understanding of the importance of critique is important. Remember that the Common Core calls for continuous peer collaboration and evaluation. The place to start learning these important skills is at home.

Details Matter

As previously mentioned, finding key ideas and details is an important skill that the Common Core ELA standards require. This standard pertains to students' work across the areas of reading, writing, and speaking and listening. Speaking and Listening standard 2 reads:

> Recount or describe key ideas or details from a text read aloud or information presented orally or through other media.

In the 1st grade, students are expected to ask and answer questions about key details in texts that are read aloud. In 2nd grade, students are asked to recount details and describe them. Recounting details requires that students listen and comprehend the story enough so as to be able to retell key ideas or details. Remember, this standard asks for the retelling of stories that are read aloud or watched using other media sources. Practice this skill by having your child retell stories that you read aloud. This will train her to pay close attention to details and will increase her comprehension levels.

As frequently noted in this book, the skills that the standards require are oftentimes connected. The standard connected to this retelling skill is Speaking and Listening standard 4, which reads:

> Tell a story or recount an experience with appropriate facts and relevant, descriptive details, speaking audibly in coherent sentences.

This standard ties in perfectly with Speaking and Listening standard 3. As your child recounts the details from the stories read aloud, ensure that she provides relevant facts and ideas in a comprehensible way.

Language Standards

There are six Language standards in 2nd grade. These Common Core standards focus on using standard English when writing or speaking. Students in 2nd grade are expected to understand how to use collective and irregular plural nouns, reflective pronouns, irregular verbs, adjectives, and adverbs. Mastering these standards will enable 2nd grade students to expand their writing pieces and use more advanced language when speaking and listening. Language standard 1 reads:

Demonstrate command of the conventions of standard English grammar and usage when writing or speaking.
a. Use collective nouns (e.g., group).
b. Form and use frequently occurring irregular plural nouns (e.g., feet, children, teeth, mice, fish).
c. Use reflexive pronouns (e.g., myself, ourselves).
d. Form and use the past tense of frequently occurring irregular verbs (e.g., sat, hid, told).
e. Use adjectives and adverbs, and choose between them depending on what is to be modified.
f. Produce, expand, and rearrange complete simple and compound sentences (e.g., The boy watched the movie; The little boy watched the movie; The action movie was watched by the little boy).

Nouns and Pronouns

This standard calls for students to understand and use collective and irregular plural nouns. Collective nouns refer to a group of things, people, or animals; for example, a herd of cattle. The term *herd* refers to all of the cattle. Your 2nd grader should start using collective nouns in his writing and when speaking. Use the following list of collective nouns to start practicing collective nouns with your child.

- A herd of cattle
- A school of fish
- A crowd of people
- A panel of experts
- A deck of cards
- A swarm of bees
- A colony of ants
- A flock of geese
- A bouquet of flowers
- A pack of wolves
- A group of people
- A bunch of grapes

Come up with other collective nouns with your child. See how many you can find when reading or watching media sources.

Irregular Plural Nouns

Children in 2nd grade should also be comfortable using irregular plural nouns. Irregular plural nouns refer to more than one object, person, or thing. What makes them irregular is that they do not follow normal rules for plurals. For instance, the plural form of *mouse* is *mice*. This does not follow typical grammar rules, which usually forms a plural by adding "s" or "es."

Ensuring that your child is familiar with these common irregular plural nouns is something you can do to reinforce this standard. The following chart provides examples of some common irregular plural nouns.

mouse	mice
child	children
foot	feet
man	men
tooth	teeth
goose	geese
person	people
woman	women
cactus	cacti

Conventions

Continue to work with your child to ensure that she is using proper conventions when writing. She should understand that proper nouns are capitalized, and she should have a grasp on when to use commas and apostrophes. These standards are highlighted in Language standard 2. Language standard 2 reads:

Demonstrate command of the conventions of standard English capitalization, punctuation, and spelling when writing.
a. Capitalize holidays, product names, and geographic names.
b. Use commas in greetings and closings of letters.
c. Use an apostrophe to form contractions and frequently occurring possessives.
d. Generalize learned spelling patterns when writing words (e.g., cage --> badge; boy --> boil).
e. Consult reference materials, including beginning dictionaries, as needed to check and correct spellings.

There are several key skills that fall under standard 2. Let's look closer at some of these skills.

Comma Use

Proper comma usage is important. Language standard 2 mentions using commas when writing notes or letters. Letter writing is an expectation for students in 2nd grade. Here is a template for writing a personal letter that you can use with your child. Be sure to reinforce the use of commas in the greeting and closing.

Dear Uncle John,
    I am so happy that we were able to visit you last week.
    I had a lot of fun learning to fish at the creek. I can't believe I caught my first fish!
    I hope we can go again next year.

Sincerely,

James

Apostrophes

Using an apostrophe to show common possessive forms is also a standard that the Common Core ELA expects of children in 2nd grade. As a reminder, this part of Language standard 2 reads:

Use an apostrophe to form contractions and frequently occurring possessives.

Possessives show that something belongs to a person or thing. Here are some common possessive forms using apostrophes.

John's book	Ann's computer
The boys' teacher	The girls' coach

You add 's if the noun ends in a consonant. If the noun ends with s you only add the apostrophe.

Spelling

As a parent, you can help your 2nd grader become skilled in using the dictionary to verify the spelling of unknown words or words with irregular spelling patterns. The more your child reads, the better her spelling will become. Reading also helps your child to use her knowledge of word spellings to review words with irregular spelling patterns.

Word Meanings

It will be important for your child to begin to recognize word meanings, including prefixes and suffixes, to figure out the meaning of unknown words. Language standard 4 addresses the key skills your child should be using to clarify word meanings. Language standard 4 reads:

Determine or clarify the meaning of unknown and multiple-meaning words and phrases based on grade 2 reading and content, choosing flexibly from an array of strategies.

a. Use sentence-level context as a clue to the meaning of a word or phrase.

b. Determine the meaning of the new word formed when a known prefix is added to a known word (e.g., happy/unhappy, tell/retell).

c. Use a known root word as a clue to the meaning of an unknown word with the same root (e.g., addition, additional).

d. Use knowledge of the meaning of individual words to predict the meaning of compound words (e.g., birdhouse, lighthouse, housefly; bookshelf, notebook, bookmark).

e. Use glossaries and beginning dictionaries, both print and digital, to determine or clarify the meaning of words and phrases.

Prefixes

Your 2nd grader should practice how to look at prefixes to determine meanings of new words. By 2nd grade your child should know these following prefixes and their meanings.

PREFIX	MEANING
re	to do again
	Example: replay
un	not
	Example: unhappy
pre	before
	Example: preview
mis	wrong
	Example: misunderstand

Compound Words

Students should be able to use their knowledge of individual words to predict the meaning of new words. Have your child look at individual word parts to determine the meaning of a word. Use the following compound word list with your child to determine word meaning.

- Snowflake
- Windmill
- Sidewalk

- Doorbell
- Snowman
- Sandpaper
- Sailboat
- Windshield
- Grasshopper
- Housetop
- Sunset
- Baseball
- Ladybug

Shades of Meaning

The final standard this chapter focuses on is Language standard 5, which reads:

Demonstrate understanding of word relationships and nuances in word meanings.

a. Identify real-life connections between words and their use (e.g., describe foods that are spicy or juicy).

b. Distinguish shades of meaning among closely related verbs (e.g., toss, throw, hurl) and closely related adjectives (e.g., thin, slender, skinny, scrawny).

Understanding the different ways to express closely related adjectives is a focus for 2nd grade students. Students at this age have a habit of using the same words over and over again. Students who have an understanding of the closely related adjectives can use them to add variety to their writing and speaking.

Let's take a closer look at part b. Understanding the different ways to express closely related adjectives is a focus for 2nd grade students. Students have a habit of using the same words over and over again. Having an understanding of the closely related adjectives can spill over into their writing and speaking.

Here are some adjectives to review with your child.

- skinny: thin, scrawny, slim
- old: ancient, aged
- fast: quick, speedy
- pretty: beautiful, gorgeous

Support Activities

There are many ways for you to help your 2nd grader master the skills detailed in these Speaking, Listening, and Language standards. Here are some additional activities you can do to help support your child.

DIRECTIONS: HAVE YOUR CHILD READ THE FOLLOWING POEM.

The Swing
By Robert Louis Stevenson

How do you like to go up in a swing,
Up in the air so blue?
Oh, I do think it the pleasantest thing
Ever a child can do!
Up in the air and over the wall,
Till I can see so wide,
Rivers and trees and cattle and all
Over the countryside—
Till I look down on the garden green,
Down on the roof so brown—
Up in the air I go flying again,
Up in the air and down!

1. What is the poem about?
2. How does the character in the poem feel?
3. What evidence from the text supports your ideas?

DIRECTIONS: HAVE YOUR CHILD USE THE WORD BANK AND WRITE THE LINKING VERB THAT BEST COMPLETES EACH SENTENCE. YOU CAN USE THE WORDS MORE THAN ONCE.

Word Bank

is are am

1. I _____ going to the park.
2. My dogs _____ fun to play with.
3. The cake _____ very sweet.
4. The girl _____ very tall.
5. We _____ going to the library.

DIRECTIONS: WRITE A SENTENCE USING EACH TRANSITION WORD IN THE WORD BANK.

Word Bank

first next then after finally

DIRECTIONS: HAVE YOUR CHILD UNDERLINE THE ADJECTIVE IN EACH SENTENCE.

1. The beautiful bird flew away.
2. There is a gigantic tree in the forest.
3. This is a very long line.
4. That quiet mouse ran away.
5. We had a delicious dinner.

DIRECTIONS: HAVE YOUR CHILD RESEARCH HIS FAVORITE PRESIDENT.

1. Have him collect at least three different sources to get information on his favorite president.
2. Have your child write a three-minute presentation on his favorite president. Have him present the presentation to you.

DIRECTIONS: SHARE THE FOLLOWING VIDEO WITH YOUR CHILD: *WWW.YOUTUBE.COM/WATCH?V=YDQEHAGJEWK*. THEN, HAVE YOUR CHILD SEARCH THE INTERNET TO FIND AN ARTICLE ABOUT THE WETLANDS.

1. After watching the video and reading the article have your child write an opinion piece about what she thinks about saving the wetlands.

CHAPTER 17

What Is Expected of Your 3rd Grade Student?

There has been a national focus on 3rd grade reading for decades. In fact, 3rd grade reading scores are used nationwide as a determining factor for future high school dropout rates. Research indicates that students not reading at grade level by the end of 3rd grade are four times more likely to drop out of school. The fact of the matter is that if students are not reading on grade level by the end of 3rd grade they will have a difficult time in the subsequent grade levels. The authors of the Common Core have included designations for phonics in 3rd grade that are designed to prepare students to read multisyllabic words and irregularly spelled words. These standards also focus on reading diverse genres of text with fluency and accuracy. This chapter delves further into Common Core standards for 3rd grade reading.

Foundational Skills

In no other grade level is it so important that students are reading with fluency and accuracy. In fact, several states have created reading laws that require schools to retain students in 3rd grade who do not pass the state reading test. The thinking behind these laws is that students who cannot read at a 3rd grade level face future consequences that are bleak.

Multisyllabic Word Reading

Reading words with multiple syllables can be quite tricky for early elementary school students. However, the 3rd grade Reading: Foundational Skills standards note that 3rd graders should be able to decode multisyllabic words.

QUESTION

What are multisyllabic words?
Multisyllabic words are words with more than one syllable. These are words like *metamorphosis*, *caterpillar*, and *telescope*.

Here is a list of multisyllabic words for 3rd grade:

3RD GRADE MULTISYLLABIC WORDS
- unhappy
- beautiful
- disappear
- kindness
- disagree
- spotless
- written
- finally
- suddenly
- thoughtfully

Chunking

One way to teach your child to read multisyllabic words is to have him chunk the words into smaller parts. For example, you can chunk the word *because* into the parts be/cause or the word *preamble* into the parts pre/am/ble. The ability to chunk words into word parts is a useful strategy that students can use as they move through the grade levels. Students in grades 4 and beyond will encounter multisyllabic words in all content areas. Increasingly complex science and social studies texts will continually challenge their reading abilities. Mastering this skill in 3rd grade is essential for meeting the demands of these higher reading levels.

ESSENTIAL

Multisyllabic words are the number-one stumbling block for struggling readers in grades 3–5. Students struggle to read these words, which hinders their ability to comprehend the text. Kids struggling with reading multisyllabic words don't know how to separate words into smaller chunks.

Fluency and Comprehension

The ability to read fluently is important for students in 3rd grade. When kids are struggling with decoding it slows down their reading, and as a result comprehension is lost. That is why mastering decoding skills in the Reading: Foundational Skills standards is so important.

As a parent, read with your child so that you can determine that she is able to read fluently. To determine your child's fluency have her read a section of a text to you. Listen to determine if her reading sounds like conversation and is not halting.

FACT

Fluency refers to the ability to read with appropriate pacing and use intonation to express meaning.

This skill is noted in Reading: Literature standard 10. Standard 10 reads:

By the end of the year, read and comprehend literature, including stories, dramas, and poetry, at the high end of the grades 2–3 text complexity band independently and proficiently.

As you probably noticed, this standard requires that students read complex texts at the 3rd grade level independently by the end of 3rd grade. To achieve this, it is essential that your child master those reading skills.

To practice, have your child read the following text aloud. Remember to listen to intonation and appropriate pacing:

Henry and Frank were excited about the new opportunity at their school. They had both been asked to create posters for the basketball tournament. Both boys liked art and could not wait to show their skills. Henry decided to draw a picture of the team that would include their team stats.

Frank was not sure what he wanted to include on his poster. He liked the idea of including the team stats, but he wanted to make his poster colorful and fun.

FACT

Reading with appropriate pace can help with comprehension. The number of words per minute a child can read has been linked to his progress on national reading assessments.

To connect reading and comprehension ask your child the following comprehension questions after reading the text:

1. What was the story about?
2. Why did Frank decide to make his poster colorful and fun?
3. What was different about the posters Frank and Henry made?

Questions to ponder after listening to your child include:

1. Did the reading sound fluent?
2. Did my child use chunking to read multisyllabic words?
3. Did my child use intonation?

As a reminder, the Reading: Foundational Skills standards require students to read more complex texts, and they will have difficulty with these texts if they are still struggling with the challenges of decoding. If you suspect that your child has any difficulty with reading, contact your child's teacher right away to see what type of extra support is available during and after school.

ALERT

These days, most schools have reading specialists on campus or in the district who can provide extra assistance as needed for students who are struggling with reading. Take advantage of these services, as they are designed to help keep your child on track for success.

Reading Literature

The reading standards for literature in the 3rd grade build on the skills students have been working on in previous grades. Students are still required to read text with the purpose of analyzing key ideas and details. Students are called to use evidence from the text to support their claims and are asked to read fables, folktales, and other fictional stories from diverse cultures. This is very similar to the requirements for 2nd graders. The only difference is that the level of text complexity is higher, and there is an increase in the precision of identifying key elements in the text that influence meaning and tone. This is referred to in Reading: Literature standard 2. Standard 2 reads:

Recount stories, including fables, folktales, and myths from diverse cultures; determine the central message, lesson, or moral and explain how it is conveyed through key details in the text.

This standard focuses on talking to students about the central message, theme, or moral of a story, fable, folktale, or myth. This is a very exciting standard because it pushes your child to think about the meaning behind the texts he is reading. Folktales and fables provide a great opportunity to discuss life lessons. For instance, the story of "The Boy Who Cried Wolf" provides an opportunity to talk about the importance of telling the truth. Here is a list of some stories, fables, and myths that you can use with your child.

Title	Message or Moral
The Boy Who Cried Wolf	Trustworthiness
The Little Red Hen	Cooperation
Little Boy Blue	Responsibility

Using Evidence from the Text

Your 3rd grader will continue to provide text-based evidence in his responses to questions that are posed. This skill is referred to in Reading: Literature standard 1. Standard 1 reads:

Ask and answer questions to demonstrate understanding of a text, referring explicitly to the text as the basis for the answers.

As noted in the preceding chapters, referring to the text is a necessity for the Common Core ELA standards. Your 3rd grader will continue to build his skills in taking information from the text to ask questions and answer them.

To help your child at home you could ask him to respond to questions that are based on texts that he is reading at school. You can get a list of the texts your child is reading in the classroom from his teacher. Perform an Internet search to find text-based questions on the text. Use those questions to work with your child on this skill.

Reading Closely

The term "close reading" is used in reference to the Common Core ELA standards. You may hear your child's teacher talking about the importance of close reading, and your child may be taught a framework or system to use for close reading. The system may involve highlighting key words in a text, rereading to clarify, and asking clarifying questions.

FACT

As a parent, here is the essence of what you need to know about close reading: Close reading refers to the skill of reading a text to get to the interpretive meaning and its nuances. The phrase "read like a detective" is sometimes used to describe close reading.

In simple layman's terms, reading closely simply means carefully reading a passage or text while delving deep into the key ideas, details, and symbolism it contains. Reading: Literature standard 3 provides an insight into close reading requirements in the 3rd grade. Standard 3 reads:

Describe characters in a story (e.g., their traits, motivations, or feelings) and explain how their actions contribute to the sequence of events.

Third graders will not be expected to do a literacy analysis. However they will be asked to make inferences about the actions of characters and the meaning behind them. To help your child with this skill, after reading a text talk with him about how the characters' actions influenced the plot development. Here are some suggested stories to use for discussing character action and plot development:

CHARACTER ACTIONS AND PLOT DEVELOPMENT TEXT SUGGESTIONS
- Paul Bunyan
- John Henry
- Johnny Appleseed
- Pocahontas
- "Casey at the Bat"

Figurative Language

Students in 3rd grade should be familiar with the use of literal and nonliteral language in texts. This skill is described in Reading: Literature standard 4. Standard 4 reads:

Determine the meaning of words and phrases as they are used in a text, distinguishing literal from nonliteral language.

Literal meanings are when words convey what they mean according to the dictionary. For example, the word *dog* means a domestic animal. However, the phrase "let sleeping dogs lie" uses the term *dog* in a nonliteral sense (the phrase means to leave well enough alone, or don't stir up trouble). Your 3rd grader will start to understand several forms of figurative language. Here is a list of some of the styles of figurative language your child may encounter.

Idiom	Group of words with a nonliteral meaning	(Let sleeping dogs lie.)
Simile	Using "like" or "as" to compare two or more unlike things	(John is as swift as a fox.)
Metaphor	Comparing two or more unlike things	(He is a shining star.)
Personification	Giving human qualities to nonliving things	(The engine sounded like a purring cat.)
Onomatopoeia	Using word sounds to suggest meaning	(The train whizzed along the track.)

Comparing Texts

The Common Core requires that your child read texts by the same author in order to compare and contrast story elements. This skill is emphasized in Reading: Literature standard 9. Standard 9 reads:

Compare and contrast the themes, settings, and plots of stories written by the same author about the same or similar characters (e.g., in books from a series).

The purpose of this standard is to allow your child to see how characters respond in different settings and how they possibly grow as the series progresses. Kids enjoy reading about familiar characters and analyzing their growth. So that your child can practice this skill, help him to find a book series or an author that he enjoys. To meet this standard he will need to compare the theme, setting, and plot of the stories.

Reading: Informational Text

Students are required to use many of the same skills they are perfecting in the Reading: Literature standards when reading informational texts. The ability to read text to answer questions using text-based evidence is the same when reading fiction or informational text. The standards are designed to help your child learn how to find key details that provide insight into the main ideas of a text. You may find that your child struggles with determining key ideas or the main idea when reading informational text. Continue to remind her that just as stories have main ideas, informational text does as well. This section focuses on a few key elements in the Common Core that differ between Reading: Literature and Reading: Informational Text so that you can better assist your child.

Cause and Effect

Your child must be able to read informational texts and understand the sequential connections between different aspects of a subject. This is outlined in Reading: Informational Text standard 3, which reads:

Describe the relationship between a series of historical events, scientific ideas or concepts, or steps in technical procedures in a text, using language that pertains to time, sequence, and cause/effect.

This is complemented by standard 8, which reads:

Describe the logical connection between particular sentences and paragraphs in a text (e.g., comparison, cause/effect, first/second/third in a sequence).

One way to help your child learn how to sequence is to go over transition words. Transition words are used to convey a sequence of events or processes. Here is a list of transition words.

First	Second	Third
Next	Last	In conclusion
Beginning	Finally	Then
At first	At last	In the end
Eventually	Over time	The next day
Afterward	Beforehand	Meanwhile

Go over the transitions as you are reading both informational and literary texts. Talk about how they are used to transition from one event or process to the next. Also encourage your child to use these transitions when speaking and writing.

Digital Text Features

The features of informational text provide clues that can help students quickly discover relevant information. Reading: Informational Text standard 5 outlines this skill. Standard 5 reads:

Use text features and search tools (e.g., key words, sidebars, hyperlinks) to locate information relevant to a given topic efficiently.

Again, we must emphasize the importance of allowing your child to talk about how different informational text features help him to understand texts. The standard mentions sidebars and hyperlinks, which are informational text features found online. To be successful in our digital age, students must understand that there are different digital text features that can help them understand key ideas and details.

As a reminder, here are the definitions of the essential features of digital text:

Key words	Bolded or highlighted words that represent key ideas
Sidebar	Found on the side of a website to indicate key information
Hyperlink	Link on websites that take you to another website or document for supporting information

Text Features

Just as digital text features are important, so are the features found in the text itself. They are referenced in Reading: Informational Text standard 7. Standard 7 reads:

Use information gained from illustrations (e.g., maps, photographs) and the words in a text to demonstrate understanding of the text (e.g., where, when, why, and how key events occur).

This standard asks your child to gain information from the graphics and illustrations used in informational texts. To practice this skill, have your child look at magazine articles and informational texts to glean information from the pictures and illustrations. Have him tell you what he can about the topic by looking at the illustrations. This is an important skill for students to develop because in the classroom they will have to use graphics and illustrations to help them understand complex ideas from informational text. Continue to support this skill with your child by pointing out the use of illustrations and graphics as you explore informational texts.

FACT

Many students skim over graphics and illustrations in informational texts. By teaching kids how to create them they will be more confident in reading them.

Comparison in Informational Texts

In the Reading: Literature standards, students are required to compare and contrast stories written by the same author in a series of books or in books that feature similar or the same characters. The standard that hits on this in informational text is Reading: Informational Text standard 9. Standard 9 reads:

Compare and contrast the most important points and key details presented in two texts on the same topic.

This standard requires that same skill of comparing and contrasting, but requires reading two different texts on the same topic. This criterion, again, supports having students conduct research on topics of interest and then finding informational texts on the topic. They then compare and contrast key details and points. Third graders should be skilled in finding key details and understanding how to use vocabulary that conveys comparing and contrasting. Review the following compare-and-contrast vocabulary words with your child.

Compare	Contrast
and, similar, alike, same, too, both	different, unlike, in contrast, but, however

CHAPTER 18

Expectations in
3rd Grade Writing

The Common Core writing standards for 3rd grade focus on precision in writing complex sentences to relay meaning. Students should be familiar with the editing process and should also have a good understanding of how to write collaboratively with peers. The concept of writing fluency is also an important aspect of the Common Core for 3rd grade. Students should be able to write without a lot of prompting and should have no trouble with writing longer pieces with minimal support. However, teacher guidance and support will still be necessary for composing informational reports and some other nonfictional writing pieces. But, at this point, students should have a strong understanding of how to write narrative pieces. This chapter focuses on the 3rd grade writing standards and the impact they have on the tasks your child will be required to complete.

Reasoning

As students get into 3rd grade they are expected to provide a list of reasons to support the arguments they write about. This skill was introduced in the 2nd grade when students were required to start using linking words to connect ideas. This skill is highlighted in Writing standard 1. Standard 1 reads:

Write opinion pieces on topics or texts, supporting a point of view with reasons.
a. Introduce the topic or text they are writing about, state an opinion, and create an organizational structure that lists reasons.
b. Provide reasons that support the opinion.
c. Use linking words and phrases (e.g., because, therefore, since, for example) to connect opinion and reasons.
d. Provide a concluding statement or section.

Third grade students must provide reasons for the conclusions they draw. This can be accomplished by writing lists or by writing text in paragraph format. Regardless, this activity can lead into teaching kids how to use transitional phrases so that they can do more than simply list their ideas.

There are numerous ways to support this skill. For example, you can provide your child with storybooks that already state opinions and provide reasons and examples to support conclusions. Some stories to consider include *I Wanna New Room* by Karen Kaufman Orloff, and *I Want a Pet Tortoise* by Gail Forsyth. In both of these stories the main characters share reasons why they want a particular item. Stories like these provide great models for kids. Read these texts and discuss them with your child. Doing so can help your child build her skills in providing evidence to support her ideas.

Another great way to support this skill is by having your child write a piece where she requests something from you, such as a later bedtime or a new toy. You can have your child write and list the reasons you should consider the request. The old adage "practice makes perfect" applies here. The more your child practices these skills, the more proficient she will become.

Illustrations and Diagrams

Students in 3rd grade should begin including illustrations and diagrams in their explanatory writing pieces. At this grade students should begin to include charts, labeled diagrams, and graphs in their work. One way to help your child understand how to start incorporating charts and graphs into her writing is to share some with her.

A few simple graph types that your child should become familiar with include:

- Bar graphs
- Pie charts
- Histograms
- Timelines
- Labeled diagrams

As you read texts, point out the use of the different illustrated graphs and diagrams. Doing this is a way to bring them to your child's attention. Before long she will probably start incorporating them into her own writing.

Facts and Opinions

Distinguishing the difference between a fact and opinion is an essential skill for students in the 3rd grade to possess. They will be given writing tasks where they are required to support an opinion using facts. Children often confuse facts and opinions. They often believe that because they think something it is a fact. Remind your child that facts can be proven, observed, or measured, and that opinions express someone's ideas, emotions, and thoughts.

ESSENTIAL

You can reinforce the difference between facts and opinions by pointing out facts and opinions in texts that you read. For instance, most any newspaper article you read will be filled with opinions. You can casually indicate facts and opinions in news stories that you read or watch to help your child begin to see the distinction.

A fun way to reinforce facts and opinions is to have your child read a short text and then list the facts and opinions that are shared. You can do this with an opinion piece from the newspaper. There are many human-interest stories on animal rescues and environmental issues that can spark a lot of debate.

Using Dialogue

Narrative writing in 3rd grade becomes more sophisticated as compared to previous grades. Students will be asked to include dialogue and description to show the feelings and emotions of characters. To support your child, it is important that you continue to expose him to fictional pieces with rich dialogue. Doing so will help him develop an understanding of how to use dialogue to express thoughts and feelings. This skill is found in Writing standard 3, which reads:

> Write narratives to develop real or imagined experiences or events using effective technique, descriptive details, and clear event sequences.
> a. Establish a situation and introduce a narrator and/or characters; organize an event sequence that unfolds naturally.
> b. Use dialogue and descriptions of actions, thoughts, and feelings to develop experiences and events or show the response of characters to situations.
> c. Use temporal words and phrases to signal event order.
> d. Provide a sense of closure.

Using meaningful dialogue that adds to the story is an important aspect of a well-crafted narrative. You may find that your child is asked to write stories that are set in multiple places. Additionally, you may find that he has an increased number of characters in his writing. Help your child think of ways to have the characters converse with one another. You can also encourage your child to think about what the characters may say if they are in different settings. For example, discuss what two friends may talk about on the playground versus what they may talk about if they are on the playground talking with their teacher.

ESSENTIAL

Children at this age are especially appreciative of the theater as they are growing in their sophistication of understanding language nuances and the use of tone and inflection to convey meaning.

Continuing to encourage your child to read rich and robust fiction and taking him to see local plays are great ways to help your child build this skill of using dialogue in his writing. Find a local children's theater and attend a weekend matinee. The experience will be wonderful and as you watch, talk about the rich dialogue used to convey meaning.

FACT

Watching live plays has been shown to be a great way to build vocabulary and comprehension. Often the language used in plays is of a higher level and the audience is required to make sense of the characters and events while watching.

Temporal Words/Transitional Words

Temporal words, or words that convey time and place, were introduced in the chapters on 1st and 2nd grade, but they are also important in 3rd grade. As a reminder, Writing standard 3 reads in part:

Use temporal words and phrases to signal event order.

Temporal words and phrases help to signal the order of events. They are important in writing, because they help ensure the events in a story flow naturally.

Writing Across Content Areas

Children in 3rd grade will be expected to write about issues in social studies, science, and more. As they are developing their writing skills the standards ask students to write about complex ideas from more demanding content sources. Writing standard 4 reads:

> With guidance and support from adults, produce writing in which the development and organization are appropriate to task and purpose. (Grade-specific expectations for writing types are defined in standards 1–3 previously given.)

Students should be familiar with writing science texts and reports. This is an activity they should have started in 2nd grade. But by 3rd grade the organization and vocabulary used in explanatory text types should be more sophisticated and have more complex development structures. This requires that your child is exposed to reading and interacting with different writing styles. As previously noted, writing and reading are connected, and children gain knowledge on how to organize their writing from the texts that they engage with. Continue to guide your child in exploring and expanding upon her existing abilities to write in different genres.

Planning, Revising, and Editing

Students in 3rd grade should be comfortable with the writing and editing cycle. This skill has been taught since kindergarten. Writing standard 5, which focuses on this skill, reads:

> With guidance and support from peers and adults, develop and strengthen writing as needed by planning, revising, and editing.

To help foster an appreciation for the editing process, continue to use writing rubrics with your child to reinforce the need to edit. Here is a 3rd grade writing rubric to use with your child:

NARRATIVE RUBRIC
- I included two or more main events
- I used sensory verbs to describe the characters and setting
- My narrative has a clear beginning, middle, and end
- My narrative has a conclusion

Digital Publication

School districts around the nation are incorporating more keyboarding instruction in their schools. As states move further into Common Core implementation this will become more prevalent. The Common Core ELA standards note that keyboarding is an important skill. This is expressed in Writing standard 6. Standard 6 reads:

> With guidance and support from adults, use technology to produce and publish writing (using keyboarding skills) as well as to interact and collaborate with others.

Continue to have your child practice keyboarding skills at home. As she moves up in the grade levels the emphasis on typing papers will increase. Here are a few websites that are appropriate for 3rd graders who are learning keyboarding skills.

- *https://sites.google.com/site/lessonfriend/3rd-grade/keyboarding*
- *www.learninggamesforkids.com/keyboarding_games/typing-factory.html*
- *www.learninggamesforkids.com/keyboarding_games/keyboarding_games_typing_adventure1.html*

Research Writing

Research is emphasized in the Common Core ELA for 3rd grade. Writing standard 7 reads:

> Conduct short research projects that build knowledge about a topic.

This is a standard you can reinforce at home. As a parent, you can encourage your child to read several sources on a topic and then write about the most important details. For a start, have your child write a short one-paragraph summary of key information on a topic that she is studying at school. This exercise will help strengthen her ability to take information and synthesize it to make sense. This skill is essential in both the workplace and college, as people are continually required to read and synthesize information and then share it with coworkers or classmates.

Note Taking

Students in 3rd grade should be skilled in taking notes to gather information from both print and digital sources. This is expressed in Writing standard 8. Standard 8 reads:

> Recall information from experiences or gather information from print and digital sources; take brief notes on sources and sort evidence into provided categories.

Understanding the key information to use in note taking can be a challenge for students in the 3rd grade. Even though students have been taking notes since the 1st grade, once in the 3rd grade they will be asked to recall information that they read during another unit of study, and then take notes about this information. Doing so requires that students remember what they learned during a previous lesson unit and connect it to what they are currently researching. As your child continues through the grade levels her ability to take good notes will become increasingly important. You can help your child with this skill. For example, you can remind your child about vacations or visits you have taken that relate to the topics being researched at school. Recalling a personal experience can help bring more clarity and interest to the subject at hand.

QUESTION

Why is note taking important?
Some students have a difficult time understanding why taking notes is an important skill to master. Note taking helps students generalize key information and then put it into their own words. It also helps them remember important facts and ideas. In addition, notes record information that can be readily accessed at a later time. As your child continues through the grade levels having a good grasp of how to take notes will become increasingly important.

Extended Writing

Students will be expected to write for extended periods of time. This is expressed in Writing standard 10, which reads:

> Write routinely over extended time frames (time for research, reflection, and revision) and shorter time frames (a single sitting or a day or two) for a range of discipline-specific tasks, purposes, and audiences.

As the standard notes, students will be expected to write over several days and also in a single sitting. By the 3rd grade, your child should be comfortable with writing and should understand the importance of coming back to a piece of writing to improve upon it and to add to it. You can encourage this practice at home by providing a focus for a writing project, setting a timer, and having your child write.

CHAPTER 19

Expectations in 3rd Grade Speaking, Listening, and Language

The Common Core standards challenge students in the 3rd grade to express themselves in oral and written forms. The language/grammar focus for 3rd grade students is on nouns and pronouns, and the proper use of commas and capitalization for titles. Students are also tasked with expanding their knowledge of root words and prefixes and suffixes to figure out unknown vocabulary words. The Speaking and Listening standards build on existing collaboration practices and expand those to include taking turns in debate and questioning strategies. Third grade students will also be asked to demonstrate that they have a firm grasp on strategies to discover meaning by asking probing questions that clarify misunderstandings. This chapter examines the speaking and listening and language skills your 3rd grader will be responsible for under the Common Core.

Preparation

By the 3rd grade students will have had experience being involved with in-group discussions. They should already have an understanding of how to find resources to share in a discussion or presentation, and know how to present their points and express information in a formal way.

Speaking and Listening standard 1a addresses these requirements. It reads:

Come to discussions prepared, having read or studied required material; explicitly draw on that preparation and other information known about the topic to explore ideas under discussion.

Students will be asked to conduct research and create note cards, or other forms of notes, to ensure they are prepared to present the information they have acquired. This may mean that your child is asked to conduct research outside of the classroom and prepare note cards.

To help your child with this expectation you can make sure that you have the resources necessary for taking notes, and help your child find the way that works best for him in preparing notes.

Some children like using note cards to jot down key points. Others like to use a sheet of paper to write out more elaborate notes. Yet others like making lists. The trick is to allow your child to explore different types of note-taking techniques until he finds the system that works best for him.

Explaining Thinking

Another key idea in the Speaking and Listening standards is explaining ideas in reference to the discussion at hand. Standard 1d reads:

Explain their own ideas and understanding in light of the discussion.

To meet this standard your child must be able to clarify his understanding so as to explain his thoughts about the subject. This can be tricky for 3rd graders, as they need time to develop the confidence to risk explaining their ideas.

ALERT

Many students are shy and don't like taking the risk of saying the wrong thing or having an idea that is different from others.

You can encourage your child to continue to build his confidence in explaining his ideas by asking for his opinions on topics. This simple strategy allows your child to express his ideas about subjects that matter to him. He will develop the language skills associated with this task and gain confidence to do so in other subjects, circumstances, and locations, including school.

A related skill is found in Speaking and Listening standard 3. Standard 3 reads:

Ask and answer questions about information from a speaker, offering appropriate elaboration and detail.

As your child develops his speaking and listening skills, he will also need to interact with his classmates and ask clarifying questions. This again is related to having the confidence to express his ideas and seek clarification of his own thoughts and the statements of others. This is a necessary skill in college and the workplace. In college your child will need to add to discussions and seek clarification, and in the workplace he will need to understand the task at hand and ask clarifying questions to ensure the job is done right.

Vocabulary

Ensuring that your child is using grade-level vocabulary is very important. Students should be using vocabulary that relates to the topics that they are studying in the 3rd grade, which include scientific information. You can help your child improve her vocabulary by having her listen to nonfiction science-related books on tape, watch scientific educational videos, and read scientific texts aloud.

Students are familiar with the vocabulary of everyday language, of course. By contrast, students must be more formally exposed to the vocabulary of subjects they are encountering in their grade. Students in the 3rd grade will encounter science and social studies topics that have challenging ideas, concepts, and vocabularies. Practicing learning strategies at home can help your child successfully engage with the science and social studies topics presented in the classroom. The following sections focus on how you can help your child with these areas of study.

Varied Media Sources

Third graders will use texts, media, and other digital sources to acquire information. It is important that they understand how to glean the most important information from these diverse sources, isolate the key ideas, interpret them, and present their discoveries.

This is a multifaceted activity that requires concentration and skill. Students have been exposed to different media sources since kindergarten, but as 3rd graders they should begin to develop skills for synthesizing information from those different sources.

Doing so requires that your child understand how to listen actively and determine key ideas across more than one source. With practice, your child can develop these skills. You can try the following activity to support this learning:

MATERIALS:
- Short text on a single topic
- Short video on the same topic
- Podcast on the same topic

PROCEDURE:
1. Tell your child he will be reading a short text, watching a video clip, and listening to a podcast of a particular topic.
2. Tell him that he should take notes as he reads and listens because you want him to summarize the information he found after he is done.
3. Have your child read the short text and take notes.
4. Have your child watch the video clip and take notes.
5. Have your child listen to the podcast and take notes.
6. Give your child time to put his notes together so he can present his findings to you.
7. Have your child tell you what he learned about the topic.

This is a great activity to use with your child. You can use it at any time to support the learning in the classroom. If your child is studying China or Westward Expansion, for example, you can find texts, short clips, and podcasts or other media sources on the topic and have your child read, watch, listen, and then talk about his findings. This will help reinforce the concepts being taught in the classroom and will also support the speaking and listening standards.

Fact Hunting

Creating an environment at home that supports exploration and learning will be important as your child progresses through the grades. Remember that the speaking and listening standards go hand in hand with the writing and reading standards.

Many students don't have the perseverance to conduct exhaustive research. For years schools have only required that students do one research paper for the year. However, Common Core standards require that students conduct research continually and build on it.

To support continual learning, consider setting up a library in your home. It can be a simple corner in the kitchen with a small bookshelf that contains a dictionary, thesaurus, and books on varied topics that your child is studying in school. You should be able to obtain a list of suggested books on the topics being studied from your child's teacher.

Don't forget that we live in a digital society, so you can always find online resources to support the topics that your child is studying in class. Having a balance of digital and paper resources is important.

What Is Relevant?

In the Common Core, students are asked to offer appropriate elaborations when asking and answering questions. In order to ask those appropriate questions students must understand what a relevant detail is. Third graders should be capable of distinguishing relevant details from those that are irrelevant. Speaking and Listening standard 2 covers relevant details. It reads:

Determine the main ideas and supporting details of a text read aloud or information presented in diverse media and formats, including visually, quantitatively, and orally.

Students are called to demonstrate this skill in their written work and oral discussions by providing appropriate details. Students will have to build on the work of their classmates and further arguments by knowing the right questions to pose. Speaking and Listening standard 3 covers elaboration. It reads:

Ask and answer questions about information from a speaker, offering appropriate elaboration and detail.

Having discussions with your child and modeling appropriate questions that add to the subject are important ways that you can support classroom learning. Watching talk show hosts as they ask probing questions can help your child see this as a model for how to ask questions to build on ideas. You can also have her listen to news interviews. A great digital source to use for this is Newsy (*www.newsy.com*). This service has great stories that are of interest to students.

Public Speaking

The authors of the Common Core ELA want to help students become comfortable speaking in public. The standards they wrote thus require that students learn to understand proper pacing and intonation when speaking. Speaking and Listening standard 4 reads:

Report on a topic or text, tell a story, or recount an experience with appropriate facts and relevant, descriptive details, speaking clearly at an understandable pace.

Students often race through their presentations due to nervousness. As your child continues to speak in public and gain confidence, her ability to speak at an appropriate rate will improve. Your child might also be asked to record herself as she creates podcasts and other digital media recordings.

This is done because it is a great way to teach appropriate pacing and tone. Speaking and Listening standard 5 reads:

Create engaging audio recordings of stories or poems that demonstrate fluid reading at an understandable pace; add visual displays when appropriate to emphasize or enhance certain facts or details.

Students love creating digital media presentations. It allows their creativity to flourish. As mentioned before, there are many great digital recording tools, like GarageBand, that your child can use to practice with at home.

Finally, speaking in complete sentences and using proper English is necessary for your child to become a truly confident public speaker. Speaking and Listening standard 6 reads:

Speak in complete sentences when appropriate to task and situation in order to provide requested detail or clarification.

This is supported by Language standard 1, which reads:

Demonstrate command of the conventions of standard English grammar and usage when writing or speaking.

The best way to model this is to correct your child when she uses slang or improper English when practicing her presentation. Also, encourage her to speak in complete sentences during regular, everyday conversations. The more practice she has with this skill, the more natural it will become for her.

Abstract Nouns

The Language standards for 3rd grade also focus on building students' ability to use nouns, verbs, and adjectives appropriately when speaking and writing. The use of abstract nouns when speaking and writing is the focus of Language standard 1. Language standard 1c reads:

Use abstract nouns (e.g., childhood).

Abstract nouns are those nouns that cannot be experienced with your senses. They represent ideas, feelings, and qualities. Examples include words like *speed*, *childhood*, and *peace*. As your child becomes more fluent in his writing and speaking he should begin to incorporate more abstract nouns into his vocabulary. Give your child the following list of abstract nouns. Ask him to add as many other abstract nouns as he can in three minutes.

ABSTRACT NOUNS
- Happiness
- Hope
- Courage
- Friendship
- Anger

This is a great exercise to help your child build his repertoire of abstract nouns. Remind him to start using these nouns in his writing and speaking activities.

Simple Verb Tense

By the 3rd grade your child should be comfortable using past, present, and future verb tense. Language standard 1e reads:

Form and use the simple (e.g., I walked; I walk; I will walk) verb tenses.

You can help your child become comfortable using simple verb tense in her writing and when speaking. Use the following chart as a reminder of past, present, and future verb tenses.

Past	Present	Future
Came	Comes	Will come
Gave	Gives	Will Give
Ate	Eats	Will Eat
Danced	Dances	Will Dance
Sang	Sings	Will Sing
Ran	Runs	Will Run
Looked	Looks	Will Look

Word Choice

Students in 3rd grade should begin to expand their vocabulary and use words for meaning and effect. This is emphasized in Language standard 3. Language standard 3 reads:

> Use knowledge of language and its conventions when writing, speaking, reading, or listening.
> a. Choose words and phrases for effect.
> b. Recognize and observe differences between the conventions of spoken and written standard English.

Encourage your child to try new words to jazz up his writing and speaking. Have him find adjectives that express feeling and tone when he speaks and writes. An activity to support this is to have your child to think of words that express various emotions or conditions. These might include:

- Words that convey fear
- Words that convey happiness
- Words that convey power
- Words that convey knowledge

See what type of words your child comes up with. As you read together, point out strong words that convey meanings and use them as a model for your child.

Support Activities

DIRECTIONS: HAVE YOUR CHILD READ THE FOLLOWING STORY. HE WILL WRITE A CONCLUSION TO THE STORY.

Elmer's New Friend
Elmer inched slowly outside the door of his house. His interest was perked when he saw a black bird walking back and forth in the yard. Elmer was not sure if the bird was waiting for a friend or if he had lost something. Elmer decided to walk over and find out what was happening. As he approached Elmer noticed

DIRECTIONS: HAVE YOUR CHILD REWRITE EACH SENTENCE WITH THE COR-RECT PRESENT TENSE VERB. THE VERBS HAVE BEEN UNDERLINED FOR YOU.

1. The women *is* going to the mall.

   _____

2. I can *ate* a big bowl of ice cream.

   _____

3. We *sitting* together on the bus.

   _____

4. My brother can *ran* very fast.

   _____

5. I like to *reading* books.

   _____

DIRECTIONS: HAVE YOUR CHILD COME UP WITH WORDS THAT CONVEY HAPPINESS, FEAR, AND SADNESS. HAVE HER RECORD THE WORDS ON A SHEET OF PAPER. HAVE YOUR CHILD THEN USE THE WORDS TO CREATE A POEM USING WORDS FROM EACH CATEGORY.

DIRECTIONS: HAVE YOUR CHILD READ THE FOLLOWING:

There are more than 5,000 kids who live in our town. Most of the kids like where we live. We have a lot of parks and fun places to go on the weekends. Last year, we learned that the city was thinking of shutting our park down. This would not be good for our neighborhood. Kids use the park to play with their friends and to spend time with their family. Every neighborhood needs a park where kids can play.

1. What facts were shared in the text?
2. What opinions were shared?
3. How does the author feel about the park?
4. What evidence from the text supports your answers?

DIRECTIONS: HAVE YOUR CHILD CONDUCT RESEARCH ON TREE SPIDERS AND TREE FROGS.

1. Have your child create a simple chart like the following one to record the similarities and differences.

Tree Spider and Tree Frog Similarities	Tree Spider and Tree Frog Differences

2. Have your child write an essay about the similarities and differences between tree spiders and tree frogs. Have your child include charts and diagrams in his essay.

CHAPTER 20

What Is Expected of Your 4th Grade Student?

Once students enter 4th grade the focus of the Common Core standards shifts from learning to read to reading to learn. This means that your child's teacher will not be teaching the basics of reading or phonics, but will instead be going into texts in depth in order to build comprehension. Fourth grade students will work with complex texts and analyze their content for meaning. The major focus of the reading standards in 4th grade is to cover strategies for reading informational and narrative texts. There are only two Reading: Foundational Skills standards in the 4th grade. They focus on reading unfamiliar multisyllabic words by using what students already know about phonics, and reading grade-level text with fluency and accuracy. If students are still struggling with decoding in the 4th grade, they will have a very difficult time comprehending the texts they encounter. In addition to the texts becoming more complex, the speaking and writing tasks will also become more challenging. This chapter discusses the expectations in reading for your 4th grader as outlined by the Common Core ELA standards.

Reading Fluency

By the 4th grade students should be reading 135 words per minute, according to national benchmarking parameters from DIBELS. Your 4th grader will also be expected to read more complex tests. Reading: Literature standard 10 expresses this expectation. Standard 10 reads:

> By the end of the year, read and comprehend literature, including stories, dramas, and poetry, in the grades 4–5 text complexity band proficiently, with scaffolding as needed at the high end of the range.

As the standard notes your child will be expected to read texts proficiently in the 4th and 5th grade text complexity band. This means that your child will be reading 5th grade texts this school year. To support this at home encourage your child to read books that are at higher Lexile levels. This will help build your child's confidence in reading complex texts.

Researchers have found that fluency rates indicate probability of reading comprehension. They have found that fluency rates correspond to increased comprehension when reading. This makes sense because when you read a text and continually have to stop to think about how to pronounce the words or what the words mean, your comprehension decreases greatly.

Many schools use sand timers or stop watches to time how quickly children read a text. Typically they set the time for one minute. It's probably not necessary to time your child when she reads, but listening to her read aloud is a good way to assess how well she is reading. Check to see if her reading has a good flow. Does she correct herself quickly when she makes errors? Does she pay attention to punctuation when reading? You can also talk to your child's teacher regarding her reading fluency. If your child is having trouble in this area you could have her read aloud with books on tape. Listening to the speaker on the tapes while reading aloud can be helpful toward improving fluency. You can also read along with your child to help practice fluency. Although schools now frown upon round robin reading, or reading aloud and taking turns, when your child enters high school and college she may be called upon to read aloud. Practicing this skill to build confidence early on is a good way to set up your child for long-term success.

Inference

The ability to make an inference from what is read is an important skill that the Common Core ELA standards require. An *inference* is when a student uses information from another source and her own personal understanding to draw a conclusion about something not explicitly communicated in the source material. This is detailed in Reading: Literature standard 1. Standard 1 reads:

Refer to details and examples in a text when explaining what the text says explicitly and when drawing inferences from the text.

Help your child understand this concept by using the following template.

The text says	
I already know	
I can infer or this could mean	

Your child can use this template to help make inferences from texts. Doing so involves using source text and what she already knows, and then drawing a conclusion.

Theme

Fourth graders should be capable of determining the theme in fictional texts. Reading: Literature standard 2 reads:

Determine a theme of a story, drama, or poem from details in the text; summarize the text.

The theme of a story is different from its plot. Sometimes students confuse the two. The theme is the overall message that the story is conveying. Remind your child that the *plot* is what the characters do and the *theme* is the message that the text is trying to show.

Popular themes in 4th grade literature include friendship, honesty, and safety.

POPULAR THEMES IN BOOKS

- **Courage:** Books where the main characters show bravery to overcome problems.
- **Perseverance:** Books where the characters do not give up under any circumstance. They keep going to accomplish their goals.
- **Honesty:** Stories where the characters prove that being honest or telling the truth is the best policy.
- **Friendship:** Stories where friendships help characters overcome obstacles.

Reinforce theme by discussing the theme or moral in the stories you read and movies you watch. Here are some guiding questions to use with your child:

1. What do you think is the theme or moral of the story?
2. What evidence can you cite from the text to support this idea?
3. Is there a lesson being taught in the text?
4. What is the lesson that the author wants us to remember?

Description

Providing in-depth or thorough descriptions of story elements is required in 4th grade. Reading: Literature standard 3 reads:

Describe in depth a character, setting, or event in a story or drama, drawing on specific details in the text (e.g., a character's thoughts, words, or actions).

The term "in depth" means that students need to go beyond simple descriptions and provide very specific and targeted descriptions of the characters, setting, and events. You can encourage this practice by asking your child to describe a family member or a favorite place using in-depth descriptions. Tell him to describe the person or place as if the listener has never seen that person or visited that place. This exercise will emphasize the importance of providing details that are relevant and help build understanding.

Take this same activity to a text by having your child describe a character from a beloved story. Have him use the same process of description he used when describing a family member. Have him go back into the text to gain more information for the description.

Making Real-World Connections

Students should begin to acquire the skill of seeing the connections between what they are reading and what is happening in the real world. By 4th grade your child should have a strong understanding of how actions relate to consequences. Having an ability to relate to the characters' actions can help students interpret the underlying meanings and themes in texts.

Encourage your child to reflect on how she connects to the characters' thoughts and actions when she is reading. This practice will assist her when she is asked to interpret the thoughts and actions of diverse characters.

It is important for students to have opportunities to explore new things. For this reason, the Common Core requires that students read texts from different cultures and regions. Sometimes finding a connection between something in another culture and something in one's own culture helps to clear up confusion and aids in comprehension.

Figurative Meanings

Understanding figurative meanings of words is a skill that 4th grade students are asked to employ. Reading: Literature standard 4 reads:

Determine the meaning of words and phrases as they are used in a text, including those that allude to significant characters found in mythology (e.g., Herculean).

Figurative language is used to provide a comparison or dramatic effect. It is words or phrases that convey a deeper meaning than their literal meanings. For example, figurative language can be expressed in phrases like, "It's raining cats and dogs" or "He has a Napoleon complex." The first example is a typical example of figurative language. In this case, you know that it is not actually raining cats and dogs, but that there is a heavy rainfall. The second example, of course, refers to the historical figure Napoleon. If students are not aware of Napoleon, then the figurative meaning of this phrase will go right over their heads.

The standard gives the example of Herculean, which means that someone is acting in strength. You know this because of your knowledge of the mythological figure called Hercules.

These figurative meanings can be very difficult for kids to catch if they are not familiar with the cultural or historical references. The ability to understand and use figurative language will continue to grow as kids go through the grade levels. Expect your child to start seeing more mythological and other historical figurative references in her texts and class assignments.

Here is a list of some common figurative references.

MYTHOLOGICAL FIGURATIVE REFERENCES

- **Herculean:** Hercules was a hero known for his strength and power. The term Herculean refers to strength.
- **Pandora's box:** According to Greek legend, Pandora's box contained evil and plagues. Today, Pandora's box refers to anything that causes trouble or strife.
- **Achilles' heel:** As a baby, the warrior Achilles was dipped into the river Styx to protect him. His heel was not dipped and it led to his downfall when he was struck in his heel by an arrow and died. If we say someone has an Achilles' heel we are referring to their weakness.
- **Nemesis:** Nemesis was a goddess of punishment and retribution. A nemesis refers to a person who is a challenge and a threat.

These are just a few Greek references; you can find a lot more on the following websites:

- *www.infoplease.com/ipa/A0934910.html*
- *http://sianaddy.weebly.com*
- *http://en.battlestarwiki.org/wiki/Mythological_references*

Genre Types

By the 4th grade, your child will have had a lot of exposure to poetry, drama, and prose. She is called to explain the major differences between the different genre types in Reading: Literature standard 5. Standard 5 reads:

Explain major differences between poems, drama, and prose, and refer to the structural elements of poems (e.g., verse, rhythm, meter) and drama (e.g., casts of characters, settings, descriptions, dialogue, stage directions) when writing or speaking about a text.

Ensure that your child has exposure to plays and poetry so that he can continue to build his understanding of the different genre types. As he reads a play draw his attention to the different features like the cast of characters and stage directions. Often, students don't pay attention to these aspects of a script, which provide a lot of detail about the play. Also, read poems to your child and talk with him about their structure. Talk, too, about the way the verses rhyme or don't rhyme, and the use of rhythm.

FACT

Reading skills like vocabulary, grammar, syllabication, fluency, and comprehension are taught through poetry. Having your child read poems is a nice way to practice fluent reading in a fun way.

You may be thinking, "Do I have to be an English teacher to do these things?" The answer is no. Don't think you have to have all the answers, but take the time to research the rhyme schemes of the poems, and the cast of characters of the plays, that your child reads. Your diligence will model and reinforce those most important perseverance skills that your child is learning in preparation for college and the workplace.

Reading: Informational Text

There are many relevant skills for reading informational and fictional texts, including the ability to find the key details and summarize key findings.

There are, however, a few other important abilities that the Common Core standards highlight.

Firsthand and Secondhand Events

In 4th grade, students are introduced to the task of comparing and contrasting information from firsthand and secondhand accounts. This skill is introduced in Reading: Informational Text standard 6. Standard 6 reads:

Compare and contrast a firsthand and secondhand account of the same event or topic; describe the differences in focus and the information provided.

First, let's distinguish the difference between firsthand and secondhand accounts.

- **A firsthand account** is a statement from someone who was actually present at or participated in a particular experience.
- **A secondhand account** is found from research or given by someone who was not there.

Examples: Firsthand	Examples: Secondhand
Diary	Textbook
Journal	Encyclopedia
Autobiography	Article
Recorded message	Handbook
Personal Interview	News story
Letter	Dictionary

Have your child read accounts of an event using a primary (firsthand) and a secondary (secondhand) source. Have your child use a Venn diagram to compare and contrast the differences in the focus and the information shared. After your child completes the exercise, discuss what she found.

FACT

We are more likely to remember information that has a personal connection. When we have a personal connection the information has deeper meaning and personal relevance. That is why when you are learning new material it helps to make connections to your previous experiences.

Interpretation of Graphs

Students in 4th grade will continue to interpret information presented in different formats to gain understanding. By 4th grade your child should be skilled in looking at graphs and charts to gain information. This is highlighted in Reading: Informational Text standard 7. Standard 7 reads:

Interpret information presented visually, orally, or quantitatively (e.g., in charts, graphs, diagrams, timelines, animations, or interactive elements on Web pages) and explain how the information contributes to an understanding of the text in which it appears.

Note that students are asked to interpret graphs and figures, which they have been doing since earlier grade levels, but now they also need to interpret information presented orally. This is an important skill to reinforce at home. As you listen to newscasts or talk-radio broadcasts, have your child discuss the information presented. Ask her what she learned from what she heard. This objective is also covered in the speaking and listening standards, which are discussed further in Chapter 22. Remember, the standards are cross-content connected.

Be sure to reinforce the importance of drawing information from graphs and figures. You can do so by having your child explain the information she gains from the graphs and charts she encounters.

Evidence

Students need to read closely to determine how an author uses reasons and evidence to support a point. This is highlighted in Reading: Informational Text standard 8. Standard 8 reads:

Explain how an author uses reasons and evidence to support particular points in a text.

This is a necessary skill for the college and career ready student. Students may have to determine the author's use of evidence and reasons, and then explain how they help to sway the reader toward a particular point of view. Strong point of view is often seen in articles on hot topics of debate. An equally strong use of reason or evidence to support that point of view may or may not be present.

The way this standard works in 4th grade is that it directs students to look for the author's use of evidence and reasons to support points in a text. You can help your child internalize this skill by having him read articles and look for the evidence and support statements that are used. The following template can be used to do this:

Point 1	Evidence and Support
Example: Eating healthy food is important.	People who eat healthy snacks have a lower risk of being overweight.
Point 2	Evidence and Support
Point 3	Evidence and Support

Good texts to use to practice this skill are magazine articles that are written about issues your child has an interest in. There are many kid-friendly magazines that include articles about things such as cell phone use, school uniform policies, and summer vacation, all which are subjects kids have opinions on. Some online resources to find such articles include the following: *www.timeforkids.com*, *www.headlinespot.com/for/kids*, *http://tweentribune.com*.

Developing Expertise

Chapter 17 discussed the importance of reading two texts by the same author in order to compare and contrast for 3rd grade students. In 4th grade students are integrating information from two texts in order to gain knowledge so they can write or speak on the topic. This skill is emphasized in Reading: Informational Text standard 9. Standard 9 reads:

Integrate information from two texts on the same topic in order to write or speak about the subject knowledgeably.

The standard notes that students should be able to speak and write knowingly on topics. Help support this by encouraging your child to become an expert on topics. As he gains expertise he will be able to speak with authority or knowingly on the topic. Here is an exercise to help your child find topics of interest:

- What do you like studying?
- What topics in school make you excited?
- What do you want to be when you grow up?
- If you could spend all day doing one thing, what would it be?
- What is your favorite place to visit?

Use these questions as a starting place for your child to help him determine what topics interest him. Encourage him to read and research these topics. As he gains knowledge have him share his new knowledge with you.

CHAPTER 21

Expectations in 4th Grade Writing

By the time your child reaches 4th grade she should have a toolbox full of strategies to use to enhance her writing. She should be familiar with different writing genres and should be able to write clearly with precision and flair. Students in 4th grade are capable of writing arguments that include sound facts and details. Their explanatory writing should incorporate graphs and figures to enhance meaning and provide clarifications. Finally, the narratives written in 4th grade should unfold naturally and not follow a scripted format. Students should begin to play with dialogue and description to enhance the story to entertain the reader. This chapter covers 4th grade writing standards and provides tips on how to help your child further hone her writing skills.

Narrative Writing

Students will be expected to write narratives that use natural language and have storylines that unfold naturally. This means that students will have to use what they know about storytelling and real life to create characters and events that are believable.

Doing so requires that your child use dialogue that is realistic and necessary to convey the ideas in the story. By this point in your child's experience in the Common Core, she will have had experience reading and writing dialogue, and she should have a pretty good grasp on how to incorporate it with better style.

Narrative writing also requires transitional phrases to help with the flow of the story. Your child should be comfortable with using phrases to connect ideas and to keep the narrative moving.

Even for seasoned writers, it isn't always easy to create believable characters that come to life for the reader. Having your child create a character map is a good way to help him build more believable characters.

Character Map #1

Name: _____ Date: _____

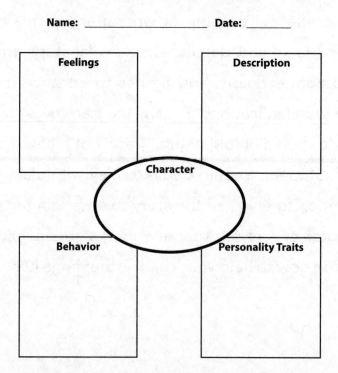

By the 4th grade your child will have had years of experience writing narrative pieces. The 4th grade writing standards provide guidance on what should be included in narrative writing pieces at this level. The presence of clear event sequencing and descriptive details are emphasized. Writing standard 3 reads:

> Write narratives to develop real or imagined experiences or events using effective technique, descriptive details, and clear event sequences.

The event sequences in your child's writing should be tight and not jump around. Oftentimes students write and have events jump from one time frame to another without precision. Remind your child that event sequences are chronological and should make sense. This relates to Writing standard 3a, which promotes letting events unfold naturally. Writing standard 3a reads:

> Orient the reader by establishing a situation and introducing a narrator and/or characters; organize an event sequence that unfolds naturally.

This again requires that your child pay close attention to his narrative writing so that the sequence of events is natural. To help your child understand this concept, have him read narrative texts while paying close attention to the sequence of events. Discuss how the event sequences unfold and if they are natural or not. This exercise allows your child to think about event sequence and its importance in writing.

The final thought to remember about narrative writing is that having well-developed characters is important. Writing standard 9a reads:

> Apply *grade 4 Reading standards* to literature (e.g., "Describe in depth a character, setting, or event in a story or drama, drawing on specific details in the text [e.g., a character's thoughts, words, or actions].").

By the 4th grade narrative writing should have more sophistication, including well-developed characters and characterizations that go beyond the obvious.

This standard asks your child to use what she is learning about dialogue, actions, and events to develop her characters and stories. This requires that students take what they are learning from their reading and then use it in their own narrative writing efforts. Encourage your child to look at the features of stories by her favorite authors, and then use them in her own writing. This will allow your child to use new techniques to enhance her narrative pieces.

Range of Writing

Students in the 4th grade are expected to be able to write for a diversity of formats. They should understand how to write prose narratives, reports, pamphlets, multimedia presentations, poetry, and other formats.

Students will be writing across content areas, and will be asked to write short responses as well as longer pieces. You can help build your child's stamina and effectiveness in writing across the curriculum. Encourage your child to ask questions about an author's intent as she reads. This will help your child to think as a writer, which can help hone her writing skills. Here are some questions to ask your child:

1. Why do you think the author chose those words?
2. How did the author help you understand the concepts?
3. What type of vocabulary did the author use to help make the meaning clear?
4. What was the author's purpose in writing this text?

Conducting Research

Because of the Common Core standards, your child has been building the skills of conducting research. In the 4th grade your child will be compiling research from multiple sources, including digital media, to write on subjects.

To research successfully, your child must categorize the topics within a subject. The subject of extreme weather, for instance, contains many categories. What is extreme weather? How does extreme weather affect people? How does extreme weather affect the environment?

Research writing helps your child learn organizational skills. She will need to keep track of the sources she finds. She will need to record the name of the source and the page number or website where she found the information. This allows your child to go back and reread or fact-check as she constructs her research report.

Students in 4th grade are required to build their skills in research writing. There are numerous standards that relate to this set of skills. The first is Writing standard 7, which reads:

> Conduct short research projects that build knowledge through investigation of different aspects of a topic.

The key point in this standard is that students should look for different aspects on a topic as they conduct research. This allows them to learn about interesting and unknown facts on a given subject. At home you can encourage your child to read multiple books so that he can determine different angles on a given topic.

The ability to take notes and provide a list of sources is important in the 4th grade. Writing standard 8 reads:

> Recall relevant information from experiences or gather relevant information from print and digital sources; take notes and categorize information, and provide a list of sources.

The list of resources that 4th graders include in their writing should be in alphabetical order and should include the author's first and last name. Check with your child's school to determine their requirements (if any) for citations.

Students should also be able to analyze and support the information drawn from literary and informational texts. This is reflected in Writing standard 9, which reads:

Draw evidence from literary or informational texts to support analysis, reflection, and research.

This means that your child should include references from the text, either fiction and/or informational text, in her research writing. This involves understanding how to find evidence to use in a writing piece. Students have been working on finding evidence and facts from texts since kindergarten, and by 4th grade they should be proficient in using facts and evidence to support their ideas.

Editing and Revising

Editing and revising become more complex tasks in the 4th grade. Because your child will be using more information in her reports, she will probably find the editing and revising process to be more time consuming. Her fact checking may require that she change sections of the text to reflect new information, or she may need to reorganize information.

ALERT

Spell check does not catch all spelling and grammar errors. Some common errors spell check often misses are incorrect pronouns, incorrect verb tense, and homonyms (words that sound the same, but are spelled differently). A great way to check a document for grammar and spelling errors is to read the text backward.

Your child should be learning these editing and revising skills in her classroom. It will be helpful to find out what type of editing marks your child's teacher is teaching so that you can reinforce them at home.

$\mathcal{e}$ = **delete**

$\wedge$ = **insert**

$\subset$ = **close space**

$\P$ = **start new paragraph**

$\equiv$ = **upper case**

$\#$ = **add space**

$\sim$ = **transpose letters**

(sp) = **check spelling**

Sample editing marks

Grammar

By 4th grade your child should have a firm grasp on how to use pronouns, verbs, and adverbs. He will use verbs to help convey meaning in his writing. For instance vivid verbs or descriptive verbs will help paint a picture for the reader. This is important as 4th graders are asked to write essays with well-chosen details.

Spelling

By the 4th grade your child should be able to correctly spell commonly confused words (for example: to, too, and two; and there, their, and they're). Your child should also be comfortable with using a dictionary to check the spelling of unknown words. Good spelling is important as your child moves through the grade levels. The best way to improve spelling is by reading. This will help your child recognize and memorize the spelling of words that can be confusing. Some words that are frequently misspelled include the following: ache, aisle, all right, awkward, banana, biscuit, breadth, buoy, buoyant, camouflage, carriage, colonel, marriage, pursue, and survey. Practice spelling these words with your child. Make it fun by having a spelling bee or having your child make flashcards to test you on the words. This repetition will help in the memorization process.

Are online dictionaries confusing for kids?
Kids must be able to look up words in a print dictionary. But as we move into the digital world, it will become increasingly important for students to access online dictionaries. There are some good online dictionaries for kids. Here are a couple of online dictionaries you can explore: *http://kids.wordsmyth.net/we* and *www.wordcentral.com*.

Typing

The Common Core standards clearly state that by 4th grade your child should be able to type a full page in one sitting. Writing standard 6 says:

> With some guidance and support from adults, use technology, including the Internet, to produce and publish writing as well as to interact and collaborate with others; demonstrate sufficient command of keyboarding skills to type a minimum of one page in a single sitting.

Allow your child to practice her keyboarding skills at home. The new-generation assessments that will assess the Common Core standards will require that students type responses to reading and writing questions. These assessments will be computer-based tests that will require students to type their responses and read texts online. This is quite different from the paper and pencil assessments that have been used for decades.

While not explicitly stated, most schools interpret a "single session," or single sitting, as one class period, meaning about one hour.

Helping to prepare your child for these tasks is important. Because children today are digital natives, adapting to keyboarding is not difficult for them. The key is that you provide your child the opportunity to practice typing skills so that he can be at ease when asked to type a one-page paper.

Clear and Focused Writing

Students in 4th grade should be able to create clear and focused writing pieces that have good development and adequate details. Writing standard 2b reads:

Develop the topic with facts, definitions, concrete details, quotations, or other information and examples related to the topic.

Students need to provide clear details to support their writing. You can help your child include clear details by asking him the following questions:

Did I provide facts?	Yes or No
Did I define important terms?	Yes or No
Were the details I provided clear?	Yes or No
Did I use quotations, examples, or other information depending on the genre I am writing?	Yes or No

Use these questions as a guide and not a checklist. They serve as a way to remind your child to include relevant details in his writing to ensure clarity.

Audience

Students in 4th grade are expected to write different types of texts to address different purposes and audiences. Students must think about task, purpose, and audience when writing texts. As your child approaches a writing piece, it is important that she think about the intended audience. She can start this process by asking, "Who am I writing for?" Remind your child to ask this question as she approaches writing tasks so that she can include the most important information for her audience and use appropriate examples and vocabulary words.

Extended Writing

Students in the 4th grade are expected to write frequently over extended time frames. Writing standard 10 reads:

> Write routinely over extended time frames (time for research, reflection, and revision) and shorter time frames (a single sitting or a day or two) for a range of discipline-specific tasks, purposes, and audiences.

This standard is echoed in subsequent grade levels, as it is important for students to concentrate on writing tasks in order for them to increase their literacy skills. This standard notes that the expectation is for students to visit and revisit their writing as they go through the editing stages.

The Common Core authors have specified that children should spend time revisiting their writing as part of the writing cycle. Editing is the focus in Writing standard 5, which reads:

> With guidance and support from peers and adults, develop and strengthen writing as needed by planning, revising, and editing. (Editing for conventions should demonstrate command of Language standards 1–3 up to and including grade 4.)

The standard notes that students should be able to use all the skills they have developed, including their knowledge of conventions, in their writing pieces. Encourage revision at home by using the following editing checklist to help your child in the editing process:

- ❑ My writing is organized
- ❑ I used complete sentences
- ❑ I used specific examples
- ❑ I used transition words
- ❑ I used vivid verbs
- ❑ I checked my spelling
- ❑ I checked my capitalization

CHAPTER 22

Expectations in 4th Grade Speaking, Listening, and Language

The speaking and listening tasks in 4th grade build on the skills that your child has been acquiring since kindergarten. Students in 4th grade will continue to be asked to participate in collaborative conversations and build on the ideas of others. They should have no trouble completing these tasks. Students in 4th grade should be very comfortable with debating and sharing their ideas in public forums. In fact, by the 4th grade students should not have to be reminded about the proper protocols of group speaking and should be pros at active listening. This chapter discusses the speaking and listening and language standards that your 4th grader will encounter.

Range of Conversations

Fourth grade students should be comfortable speaking in different formats. Speaking and Listening standard 1 reads:

> Engage effectively in a range of collaborative discussions (one-on-one, in groups, and teacher-led) with diverse partners on grade 4 topics and texts, building on others' ideas and expressing their own clearly.

The ability to speak and share information in small and large group settings is an important college and career skill. Students will continue to build their confidence and craft in this area during the 4th grade.

Continue to encourage your child to practice public speaking whenever you can. Some children are very shy and need a lot of encouragement to get up and talk in front of groups. Be patient with your child as she develops this important skill set. If your 4th grader continues to struggle with oral presentations, have a discussion with your child's teacher. Work together to come up with a plan to make this task less stressful for your child. Perhaps your child could practice her presentations with the teacher before she presents in front of the class. This way the teacher is able to offer suggestions that may help your child be less stressed when she is called upon to speak in class.

Interpreting Charts and Graphs

Your 4th grader will be asked to explain information obtained from diverse media formats. These formats can include charts and graphs and other visual displays. Being comfortable explaining technical information found in charts and graphs can be quite challenging. This skill will build across the grade levels, but your child should start to practice it in the 4th grade. Speaking and Listening standard 2 reads:

> Paraphrase portions of text read loud or information presented in diverse media and formats, including visually, quantitatively, and orally.

You can help your child by looking at infographics and talking about the information that is presented visually.

Infographics are visual representations of information. They incorporate images and graphics to present information. Here is a great website with examples of infographics: *www.loveinfographics.com/categories/political-infographics/how-laws-are-made-infographic-infographic.*

As your child becomes more familiar with interpreting visual displays, this knowledge will spill over into his own presentations. Continue to encourage the understanding of visuals and graphics, and how to discuss their contents orally.

Expressing Key Ideas

Students should be comfortable articulating the key ideas they encounter in their reading and when listening to others. Speaking and Listening standard 1d reads:

Review the key ideas expressed and explain their own ideas and understanding in light of the discussion.

Students in 3rd grade are asked to explain their own ideas, but once they get to 4th grade they are expected to review the key ideas they expressed as well as explain their understanding. This involves providing the listener with an explanation of the key points in an oral discussion. Students have already performed this task by way of the writing and reading standards from the earlier grades, but in 4th grade they will extend this task into the speaking and listening standards. Work with your child so that she is able to articulate key points when she forms an opinion. She will be able to transfer this skill to the classroom.

Pacing and Tone

Students should be comfortable speaking in public, and speak with an appropriate pacing and tone to keep their audience engaged. Speaking and Listening standard 4 reads:

> Report on a topic or text, tell a story, or recount an experience in an organized manner, using appropriate facts and relevant, descriptive details to support main ideas or themes; speak clearly at an understandable pace.

Speaking at a pace that is understandable and appropriate is a skill that is developed with practice. Some children are gifted with the ability to talk at a pace that is upbeat and not monotone. Some children struggle with this and fumble or drag their words along. You can help your child by providing good models from any number of digital media sources. Such examples are great ways to help him understand how important pacing is. Also have your child record himself presenting on a topic. A careful review of his performance will help him discover ways to improve his pacing. Remind your child of the following:

- Slow down
- Pronounce all words
- Take a breath between sentences
- Give eye contact
- Smile
- Relax

These tips will help your child be more aware when he is presenting so that he can clearly articulate his message. The ability to articulate messages in a clear way that is well paced is a valued skill in both college classrooms and the workplace.

Visual Displays

Student reports should be more technologically savvy by the 4th grade. Including media and visual displays to spice up a presentation is an expectation for 4th graders. Speaking and Listening standard 5 reads:

Add audio recordings and visual displays to presentations when appropriate to enhance the development of main ideas or themes.

Students can enhance their presentations through the use of music, video clips, and audio clips. You may find that your 4th grade child is starting to use more tech features in her reports and presentations. Being up-to-date on current technology will help keep you in the loop. Technology is ever-changing and it changes quite rapidly. The fact is, your child may become more of an expert than you on many of the new technologies. As a parent you should be willing to learn from your kids and be there to support them when they need you.

Formal and Informal English

Distinguishing when to use formal and informal English is another skill that students need to learn. They will need to determine the task and audience to figure out whether formal or informal speech is appropriate.

ESSENTIAL

Knowing whether to use formal or informal English can be a difficult task for 4th graders to understand. They are typically most comfortable using informal speech and often fall back into informal speech when presenting.

You can help your child determine when to use formal or informal speech by reminding her to reflect on the purpose of the presentation and the intended audience. Remind your child that formal speech is used when talking with a person of authority or presenting formal information. By contrast, informal speech is appropriate when talking to friends or on the playground. As your child improves her presentation skills, any tendency toward reverting to informal language should decrease.

Modals

Modal verbs are used to express possibility or obligation. Children oftentimes struggle with using modal verbs, especially if they rely on slang or do not have proper English models. Here is a list of modal verbs.

can	could	may	might
would	must	will	should

EXAMPLES:
- He can speak Spanish.
- She should be home by 8:00 P.M.

The use of "not" makes modal verbs negative.

EXAMPLES:
- She should not be angry.
- He may not come to the park.

Prepositional Phrases

Fourth graders should be comfortable using prepositional phrases when speaking. A prepositional phrase is a group of words that includes a preposition, its object, and any of the object's modifiers. For example, for the phrase "in the park," the word "in" is the preposition, and "the park" is the object that something is in. Here is another example: In the phrase "to the store," the word "to" is the preposition, and "the store" is the object. As your child is speaking make sure that he is using prepositional phrases properly to help reinforce this skill.

FACT

Grammar and usage are as important in oral communication as they are in written communication. Many students have no trouble writing using correct grammar, but fall into slang when speaking.

Vocabulary

Students in 4th grade should be building their academic vocabulary in the different content areas. Language standard 6 reads:

Acquire and use accurately grade-appropriate general academic and domain-specific words and phrases, including those that signal precise actions, emotions, or states of being (e.g., quizzed, whined, stammered) and that are basic to a particular topic (e.g., wildlife, conservation, and endangered when discussing animal preservation).

Vocabulary building is imperative. Because the complexity of the texts your child reads is increasing, she will encounter and be expected to use more difficult, content-specific language. The example in the standard involves using words like "wildlife," "conservation," and "endangered" when writing or speaking about wildlife. As your child conducts research and learns about new topics the expectation is that she will use those new vocabulary words confidently to complete work tasks.

FACT

You can support vocabulary building at home by having your child keep a notebook where she lists new words she finds while learning about a new topic. Your child can refer to this personal dictionary when writing and speaking about new topics. Keeping such a dictionary will help her to quickly acquire new vocabulary words and start using them with confidence.

Concise Language

Using the right words and phrases to convey meaning is a skill your 4th grader should work on. Language standard 3a reads:

Choose words and phrases to convey ideas precisely.

This standard asks that students use great precision when choosing the words in their written reports and when speaking. The words they choose should convey the appropriate meaning and message. The Common Core standards help students to become accustomed to using appropriate word choices in their writing narratives, but when writing or speaking about informational topics this can be a struggle for them.

The language of nonfiction differs from that of narrative fiction. Students will be asked to use vocabulary related to the topic they are discussing, and often these words are scientific or technical. It is important that you help your child understand how to use resources to clarify meaning of unknown words. Language standard 4c reads:

Consult reference materials (e.g., dictionaries, glossaries, thesauruses), both print and digital, to find the pronunciation and determine or clarify the precise meaning of key words and phrases.

Encourage your child to use dictionaries, both digital and print, when he encounters words that he struggles with. Developing this habit will help him build his vocabulary and strengthen his ability to incorporate new words into his speaking and writing. Often students struggle with the vocabulary of science, which hinders their ability to clearly articulate their knowledge when giving presentations. Encouraging your child to read science materials and articles is a good first step toward helping him overcome this struggle. Also, as your child prepares a presentation on a particular topic, ensure that he has adequate resources that provide models of language and vocabulary that he should then use in his work.

Antonyms and Synonyms

Students should be able to clarify their understanding of vocabulary words by relating words to their opposites and equivalent words. Language standard 5c reads:

Demonstrate understanding of words by relating them to their opposites (antonyms) and to words with similar but not identical meanings (synonyms).

One way you can help your child gain a clear understanding of a word is to ask her to tell you a synonym and an antonym for the word. Synonyms are words with the same meanings. Antonyms are words with the opposite meaning of a given word. For example:

Word	Synonym	Antonym
happy	glad	sad

Have your child think of synonyms and antonyms for the following words:

Word	Synonym	Antonym
Sad		
Long		
Brave		
Hot		
Cold		
Round		

Impress upon your child the idea that knowing a synonym and an antonym of a word helps her build understanding of the word's actual meaning and underlying meanings. As your child acquires new vocabulary this is an easy way to help her expand her learning.

Support Activities

DIRECTIONS: HAVE YOUR CHILD USE THE WORD BANK AND WRITE THE PRONOUN THAT BEST COMPLETES EACH SENTENCE.

Word Bank
his they our her he

1. _____ rode his bike to the park.
2. She left _____ book at school.
3. My family painted _____ house this weekend.
4. _____ studied day and night for the test.
5. Dad wrecked _____ motorcycle.

1. The boys _**seen**_ a bear.

   _____

2. The cat _**sleeped**_ all day.

   _____

3. We _**washt**_ the dishes for mom.

   _____

4. The window _**breaked**_ into pieces.

   _____

5. My sister _**climbt**_ the tree.

   _____

DIRECTIONS: HAVE YOUR CHILD READ THE FOLLOWING WORDS. CIRCLE THE ADVERBS.

dog	slowly	television
happily	run	fight
sit	pillow	quickly
beautifully	computer	walk
game	quietly	dance

DIRECTIONS: HAVE YOUR CHILD UNDERLINE THE PREPOSITIONAL PHRASE IN EACH SENTENCE.

1. The clouds float through the sky.
2. The girls rushed into the mall.
3. My family got on the airplane.
4. Many houses were underwater during the flood.
5. He learned a lot about animals in science class.

DIRECTIONS: HAVE YOUR CHILD DRAW A LINE FROM EACH WORD TO ITS ANTONYM.

loving	fake
wealthy	humble
brave	fearful
prideful	poor
real	hateful

DIRECTIONS: HAVE YOUR CHILD READ EACH SENTENCE. MARK EACH SENTENCE WITH "S" IF IT IS A SIMILE OR "M" IF IT IS A META-PHOR.

1. The girl ran as fast as a horse. _____
2. Mom told me I had to be as quiet as a mouse. _____
3. Our house is a zoo! _____
4. My brother laughs like a monkey. _____
5. That teacher is a bear. _____

CHAPTER 23

What Is Expected of Your 5th Grade Student?

The Reading: Foundational Skills standards end at the 5th grade. Students typically no longer receive classroom instruction on phonics and fluency after leaving the 5th grade. Children should be comfortable with figuring out unknown words by using syllabication and word clues like context and word parts. As well, students in the 5th grade should have a firm grasp on reading with fluency and accuracy, and be able to read complex science, social studies, and technical texts independently and with confidence. This chapter covers the 5th grade expectations in reading, and also provides some tips to help your child master these skills.

Context and Comprehension

By the time your child enters 5th grade he should have a pretty hefty set of tools to help him figure out unfamiliar words. The fact is, when reading complex technical and scientific articles your child will run across words that are unfamiliar. Of course, students have the dictionary as a tool, but often children can use the context or frame of the sentence to figure out the meaning of an unknown word.

FACT

Context clues are information—such as synonyms, antonyms, definitions, or examples—that are near an unknown word. These clues can be used to figure out the meaning of that word.

To figure out the meaning of an unknown word using context, your child can replace the word with a word she knows to see if it makes sense in relation to the context of the sentence. Let's use the word *poverty* in an example sentence: "Mary did not have much money and was in extreme poverty." Looking at the context of the sentence your child could figure out the word poverty means poor, as in lacking money.

Help your child use context to figure out unknown words the next time you are reading together.

Morphology

Students in 5th grade should have a good understanding of the two types of word parts: roots and affixes. A root is the part of a word that comes from another language. Most typically in English that other language would be Greek or Latin. An affix is a word part that when attached to a root (or base word) creates a new word. Short words like *speak* and *solve* are base words. An affix can be a prefix that comes at the beginning of a word, or it can be suffix that comes at the end of a word. Here are some common affixes:

Affix (prefix)	meaning	affix (suffix)	part of speech
bi-	two	-al	adjectival suffix
anti-	against	-fy	verb suffix
inter-	between	-ic	adjectival suffix
pre-	before	-ion	noun suffix
super-	above	-ism	noun suffix
trans-	across	-ize	verb suffix
dis-	not	-ous	adjectival suffix

Another way to determine the meaning of unknown words is to look at their word parts and find common meanings. For example, if you know that the root *tele* means far or across a distance, then you can use this information to determine that *television* means to see a picture from a distance, and *telescope* means to see things in the distance.

ESSENTIAL

Studies have found that when students have a large working vocabulary their reading comprehension scores increase. Encouraging your child to continue to learn new vocabulary is increasingly important in 5th grade and beyond.

Rereading

As your 5th grader wrestles with increasingly complex texts, it is important that she understand that rereading is often necessary for comprehension. Reading: Foundational Skills standard 4c reads:

Use context to confirm or self-correct word recognition and understanding, rereading as necessary.

Oftentimes, kids don't understand that rereading is a good thing and not an indication of something negative. Encourage your child to reread sections of text that are confusing to her or that contain difficult vocabulary. Model this yourself when reading technical manuals. We know that fluency and comprehension go hand in hand, but comprehension is the purpose for reading. A child can read with fluency and elegance, but if he does not understand the words on the page, then the entire exercise is for nothing.

The authors of the Common Core use the phrase "rereading as necessary" to remind us that rereading is an important part of comprehension. It is most important that your child understand that re-reading is a part of the reading process and is in fact a sign of a good reader. Stress the importance of re-reading as it helps to clarify meaning and helps the reader comprehend complex ideas. As your child becomes more familiar with reading informational text the need to re-read sections should decline.

QUESTION

What is the best way to take notes when reading a text?
Many students take notes in the margins of their books or highlight when they read a text. Sometimes this is not an option if you are using a library book or a book from the school. In these cases using sticky notes is a nice way to take notes. Have your child place the sticky notes on the areas in the text where he wants to make notes. You can buy regular-sized sticky notes and cut them into manageable strips so that they can be placed along the side of the book.

Quoting from Text

Students in 5th grade should begin quoting evidence from a text. Reading: Literature standard 1 reads:

Quote accurately from a text when explaining what the text says explicitly and when drawing inferences from the text.

Students often struggle with how to accurately quote from a text. Fifth graders can use any number of sophisticated phrases to express quotations with accuracy. Here are some ideas:

- According to the text . . .
- On page 12 the author states . . .
- According to the author, John Smith . . .
- In the article "Kids Matter," the authors state . . .

Have your child play around with different ways to use quotes from the text. Challenge your child to use different statements so that she can increase her repertoire. She can also find models of how to quote by reading nonfiction articles and seeing how other authors quote citations.

Character Analysis and Interaction

Analyzing characters' actions and responses to challenges is an important skill that 5th graders will work on. Reading: Literature standard 2 reads:

Determine a theme of a story, drama, or poem from details in the text, including how the characters in a story or drama respond to challenges or how the speaker in a poem reflects upon a topic; summarize the text.

Looking carefully at a character's growth throughout a text is very important for this analysis. Fifth graders should begin to ask questions about what motivates characters to respond in the manner that they do. For instance, when faced with adversity how does the character react? Does she run and hide or does she persevere and overcome the challenge? Students should have a keen understanding of how behaviors reflect inner emotions and motivations. Students will be asked to respond to questions about characters' motives and transformation.

FACT

To move beyond basic characterization of characters encourage your child to think about key motivation and ethical dilemmas when discussing characters. It may take some prompting on your part, but continue to ask why did the character act they way he or she did? Also remind your child to give specific evidence from the text in her response.

Support this at home by talking about characters in books and movies. Discuss how they change over the course of time. For example, look at how the hero of a story or movie starts out being weak and afraid, but ends up being brave and wise by the end. Discuss what happens to help characters change. Some good books to consider using when working on this standard include *Anne Frank: The Diary of a Young Girl*, *Bud, Not Buddy*, and *Esperanza Rising*. All of the aforementioned stories have characters that encounter obstacles that will be appropriate for 5th graders to understand and discuss.

Character Interaction

Being able to compare and contrast is important because it helps students organize both old and new information. This skill will become increasingly important as students move into middle school and high school. In those grade levels students will be asked to conduct comparisons of increasingly demanding content. The Common Core standards help 5th grade students learn to compare and contrast events, settings, and characters. This skill is highlighted in Reading: Literature standard 3, which reads:

Compare and contrast two or more characters, settings, or events in a story or drama, drawing on specific details in the text (e.g., how characters interact).

This standard requires that students closely read texts to determine how the story elements (characters, settings, and events) compare. The standard gives an example of character interaction. Your 5th grader will begin building this skill by comparing and contrasting the interactions between characters in a story. To analyze these interactions your child will look at dialogue and personal interactions between the two characters. Upon completing an analysis your child will draw conclusions about character traits and character growth. The ability to compare and contrast using different story elements is an important thinking skill that will help your child to critically analyze subjects in both the workplace and in school.

Narrator Focus

Students have learned to look for an author's point of view when reading informational text. This is also important to do when reading fiction. Reading: Literature standard 6 reads:

Describe how a narrator's or speaker's point of view influences how events are described.

This is a very important standard, because it pushes your child to think about the word choice and details that an author chose to create the mood of a story. This standard gets into the practice of using words to convey emotions and colors to represent emotions. These are the beginning steps of sophisticated literary analysis. Such analysis requires students to look at text in a deliberate manner to draw out the nuances in the language used. This skill is not mastered overnight, and is a struggle for some, as it requires thoughtful reflection on the intended purpose behind the words and examples chosen in a text.

Here are some words that are often used in text to evoke emotion:

Words and Phrases Used to Evoke Positive Emotions	Words and Phrases Used to Evoke Negative Emotions
Pleasant	Harmful
Boost	Had Enough
Cure	Temporary
Energize	Conspiracy

Have your child complete a list where he writes words and phrases that evoke positive and negative emotions. This will prove to be a good exercise in teaching your child to look for these words when reading.

ESSENTIAL

You can help your child hone the skill of describing the author's point of view by having him discuss the music that is used in films to convey emotion. You can watch movies and talk about the use of music to convey happiness, intensity, and fear. Your child can transfer that knowledge into the texts that he is reading.

Graphic Novels

Graphics and visuals are important literary elements that work to convey meaning in stories. They are engaging and provide vibrant pictures to help further the author's meaning. Reading: Literature standard 7 reads:

Analyze how visual and multimedia elements contribute to the meaning, tone, or beauty of a text (e.g., graphic novel, multimedia presentation of fiction, folktale, myth, poem).

Kids love graphic novels. Graphic novels are a form of comic books. They are very popular with kids in grade 4 and up. This standard asks kids to analyze how the visuals used in books like graphic novels help convey meaning and tone. Have your child discuss the illustrations in graphic novels, folktales, multimedia presentations, and storybooks. Discuss how these graphics help the reader understand the text better. Oftentimes the graphics help to depict characters' feelings and emotions. Think about the comic books you may have read as a child. It was probably just as much fun to look at the pictures as it was to read the text. Seeing the characters' faces and reactions helped you understand and experience the meaning and emotions of the story. This is exactly what this standard is asking kids to do. As students read graphic novels or multimedia works, they should pay attention to the graphics to determine mood and meaning. Practice this important skill with your child the next time you are reading a comic or graphic novel.

Informational Text

There are several important skills that the Common Core standards help 5th grade students develop in regard to reading informational text. This section will focus on some key skills and ideas that you can reinforce at home.

Quoting

Students in 5th grade should become increasingly skilled in quoting from texts. This is emphasized in Reading: Informational Text standard 1, which reads:

Quote accurately from a text when explaining what the text says explicitly and when drawing inferences from the text.

To meet this standard, students must comprehend the meaning of the text and include an accurate quote to convey this meaning in the context of their own work. This can be tricky because it requires that the child both understand the quote she is going to share and also relate it to the explanation she is providing. This standard goes a long way in helping students understand the importance of accurately quoting, as they will likely notice that accurate quotes provide strength to their written and spoken arguments.

Relationships

Finding the relationship between events and ideas is an important skill that children in 5th grade must master. Reading: Informational Text standard 3 reads:

> Explain the relationships or interactions between two or more individuals, events, ideas, or concepts in a historical, scientific, or technical text based on specific information in the text.

This standard calls for students to discuss the relationship of two or more historical, scientific, or technical events. For example, when surgeons wash their hands before surgery, the occurrences of patients contracting diseases after surgery decrease. Students will be reading a vast amount of information in science, history, and technical areas. They will need to hold on to information and discuss how events and discoveries affect outcomes. The power in this standard is that it allows students to determine cause and effect relationships. Understanding these causal relationships between events is important when making decisions, hypothesizing, and problem solving.

This standard is related to Reading: Informational Text standard 6, which reads:

> Analyze multiple accounts of the same event or topic, noting important similarities and differences in the point of view they represent.

This standard asks kids to analyze the events or topics from different sources and note the similarities and differences. Students did this in 4th grade when they were asked to compare and contrast firsthand and secondhand accounts. The 5th grade standard does not specify if the sources have to be firsthand or secondhand but requires that students analyze different sources' accounts of the same event. You can practice this with your child by having him read news articles on a topic. He can discuss how the event or topic is presented in each news article. This is a great exercise for your child to increase his analytical skills.

Finding Information

The ability to locate information to answer questions is extremely important. This ability to access information quickly and effectively will prove an important skill to have. This skill is the focus of Reading: Informational Text standard 7. Standard 7 reads:

Draw on information from multiple print or digital sources, demonstrating the ability to locate an answer to a question quickly or to solve a problem efficiently.

The key word in this standard is "quickly." This standard asks that kids locate information in an efficient manner to answer questions or solve problems. Your child will need to develop skills in locating important information. To do so, your child must be able to use headers, glossaries, and indexes to quickly assess information. In the digital arena it means knowing how to quickly conduct searches and locate the needed information in a timely manner. Continue to support your child as she works to build her skills for finding answers quickly.

CHAPTER 24

Expectations in 5th Grade Writing

Taking notes and keeping up with research are common practices for students in 5th grade. They have had years of experience with research writing and should be pros at gathering information and categorizing it. Students should also have a clear understanding of what good writing looks like, and they should be incorporating those characteristics into their own writing. Expect to see a lot of revisions of work and more demanding writing assignments in the 5th grade. Fifth graders should be able to write research reports that include numerous references, and they should have no problem incorporating facts and figures into their nonfiction writing pieces. This chapter will focus on the writing standards for the 5th grade and what you can expect from your 5th grader.

Revision, Revision, Revision

The only way for students to improve their writing is to engage in the revision process. Revisions will be frequent and should be expected. Students in 5th grade may have to revise a piece of writing three to five times before it is in an acceptable form. Writing standard 5 reads:

> With guidance and support from peers and adults, develop and strengthen writing as needed by planning, revising, editing, rewriting, or trying a new approach.

The editing process is not intended to frustrate the child, but to allow for critique and targeted improvement. The revision process for 5th grade students should involve several rounds of revision that focus on different aspects of the writing that need improvement. If you give too much feedback at one time you run the risk of overwhelming your child. It's better to provide measured feedback so that your child can gain confidence in one area before moving on to the next.

Encourage your child to take the revision process in stride and use it as a learning tool to improve her writing. Use writing rubrics to help your child examine her writing pieces for improvement. Here is a writing checklist that can be used for 5th graders.

- ❏ My topic is focused
- ❏ I have a beginning, middle, and end
- ❏ My writing has a logical sequence
- ❏ I used specific details to enhance my writing
- ❏ I used paragraphs to help my writing flow
- ❏ I used transition words as needed to enhance my writing
- ❏ I used description as needed to enhance my writing
- ❏ I checked my spelling and grammar

Writing Arguments

Fifth graders should be able to write arguments that have a strong structure in place. The argument should be introduced by stating their stand on the issue and the subsequent ideas should flow logically. The conclusion should be related to the opinion stated and have a natural closing.

Your child will have done work with writing arguments since kindergarten. In 5th grade he will put together all that he has learned about using transitions, using evidence-based reasons, and logically grouping topics and ideas. Writing standard 1 reads:

> Write opinion pieces on topics or texts, supporting a point of view with reasons and information.

To help your child with this standard, have him state his opinion on social issues. Ask your child to clarify why he is taking the stand he is. Finally, ask him to sum up his stance. By having your child orally articulate his stance on issues he can further internalize the structure for well-developed arguments/ opinion pieces.

When choosing topics for argument writing it is important to pick a topic that can be debated. Often students pick topics that have limited points of view and are not complex enough for a good debate.

Writer's Craft

Students in 5th grade will write informative texts and narratives. This will be nothing new for 5th grade students, but the writing is at a higher level of expectation. For example, your child's informative piece should be logical and should include illustrations, charts, and lists that help enhance a reader's understanding of an idea. Writing standard 2 reads:

> Write informative/explanatory texts to examine a topic and convey ideas and information clearly.

This means that your child should use precise language that aids in understanding. Precise language refers to the ability to give specific responses. Often students want to give generalized explanations or quick summaries. When they use precise language they are required to provide thoughtful commentary that enhances the topic.

Writing standard 2a states:

Introduce a topic clearly, provide a general observation and focus, and group related information logically; include formatting (e.g., headings), illustrations, and multimedia when useful to aiding comprehension.

The standard clearly denotes that formatting is important when constructing explanatory texts. Students should be familiar with the layout of explanatory documents like articles, brochures, and pamphlets. Provide your child with access to these different types of documents so she can have some models to use and incorporate in her writing tasks.

A Narrative Is Just a Narrative, Right?

Writing narratives for 5th graders should be a piece of cake. They have been reading stories and writing narratives for years. The bar is raised in the 5th grade in that students are asked to bring in situations and introduce narrators and characters. Writing standard 3a reads:

Orient the reader by establishing a situation and introducing a narrator and/or characters; organize an event sequence that unfolds naturally.

This is a far cry from the typical stories that students have been writing up to this point. No longer can they just write a fun story about a day at the park. Students are now asked to get into character analysis and plot development. At this point, students have been reading rich literature, including the classics. Thus, writing about characters and creating situations that promote character development is something that your child should be able to grasp.

Students in 5th grade also focus on using dialogue and pacing to help enrich their narrative writing. Writing standard 3b reads:

Use narrative techniques, such as dialogue, description, and pacing to develop experiences and events or show the responses of characters to situations.

Continue to read classic literature with your child and discuss characters and plots as they relate to character development. As your child reads, ask her how she thinks she can use these same story elements in her own writing. This will help encourage your child to incorporate these literary elements to strengthen her writing.

QUESTION

Should I still read texts aloud to my 5th grader?
Yes, reading aloud is a great way to spend time with your kids and it also encourages a love for lifelong reading. As your child prepares for college and career success, the need to be a lifelong reader is imperative. He will continually read new journals and training manuals to keep up in his job, and in college reading will be necessary in all subject areas.

Task, Purpose, and Audience

Student writing should appropriately match the task, purpose, and audience. Writing standard 4 reads:

Produce clear and coherent writing in which the development and organization are appropriate to task, purpose, and audience. (Grade-specific expectations for writing types are defined in standards 1–3 discussed previously.)

Students have had practice with this in their speaking and listening tasks. This knowledge should transfer over into their writing, and they should be able to produce pieces that use appropriate language, tone, and organization.

ALERT

Tone and mood are very similar. Students sometimes confuse the two. Tone refers to the attitude of the author. This is conveyed through the words used; for example, "I would rather starve then eat your cooking." Mood refers to the overall feel of the text. An example would be, "It was a dark and gloomy night."

A fiction piece will use different language than a research paper. Students in 5th grade should have a firm understanding of how to switch their writing tone and focus as needed.

Flexibility

As mentioned previously, revising will be a necessary function of writing in the 5th grade. Students will also need to be flexible in their approach. Writing standard 5 reads:

With guidance and support from peers and adults, develop and strengthen writing as needed by planning, revising, editing, rewriting, or trying a new approach.

Being open to trying a new approach to a writing task will be important for your child. Being open to other ways of doing things is important as the tasks he is being asked to complete become more sophisticated. For example, using a different style for a narrative or adding graphics to enhance a factual piece may improve the work. Encourage your child to try new ways of writing so he doesn't get into a rut. Make trying new writing styles an adventure.

Technology

Students in 5th grade should be able to write with a keyboard a minimum of two pages in a single sitting. As noted previously, a single sitting is not clearly defined, but probably constitutes a class period of sixty minutes. Continue to encourage your child to improve on his keyboarding skills by having him practice typing at home.

Writing standard 6 reads:

With some guidance and support from adults, use technology, including the Internet, to produce and publish writing as well as to interact and collaborate with others; demonstrate sufficient command of keyboarding skills to type a minimum of two pages in a single sitting.

Continue to encourage your child to write using technology. As the grade levels increase, your child will be required to write using technology more frequently. By the 5th grade, your child should already have basic keyboarding skills and should be comfortable typing papers on a computer or other digital devices.

Clear Focus

Fifth grade writing should have a clear organizational structure that has a logical flow. Writing standard 1a reads:

Introduce a topic or text clearly, state an opinion, and create an organizational structure in which ideas are logically grouped to support the writer's purpose.

As the standard notes, student writing should be grouped into categories that are logical and help support the organizational structure of a piece. This is a hallmark of informational writing. Remind your child to look at how her topics are grouped together so that the reader can easily understand the information.

This logical organization also refers to supporting details and facts. Writing standard 1b reads:

Provide logically ordered reasons that are supported by facts and details.

This standard requires that the reasons students use in their writing are logically placed so as to clarify understanding. Encourage your child to use outlining to determine where to place her facts and examples. Here is a sample outline that you can use with your child to encourage her to think about the organization of her writing and determine where the key facts fit.

INTRODUCTION
- Fact 1 and supporting details
- Fact 2 and supporting details
- Fact 3 and supporting details
CONCLUSION

Research Writing

Research writing will be nothing new for your 5th grader. Students in 5th grade will continue to develop their skills in writing research texts. Writing standard 7 reads:

> Conduct short research projects that use several sources to build knowledge through investigation of different aspects of a topic.

Your child should be comfortable using multiple sources in his research papers. These sources should help to build knowledge and provide adequate details to support the research topic. Another important skill needed for research writing is summarizing information from diverse sources. Writing standard 8 reads:

> Recall relevant information from experiences or gather relevant information from print and digital sources; summarize or paraphrase information in notes and finished work, and provide a list of sources.

This standard calls for students to have the ability to gather information from diverse sources (digital and print) and write notes that paraphrase key ideas. By the 5th grade, your child should already be a pretty good note taker. You can help you child build on this skill by having him read short excerpts of text, and then write notes on a note card. Building this skill will enable your child to conduct research effectively.

The final writing skill this chapter will focus on is drawing evidence. Writing standard 9 reads:

Draw evidence from literary or informational texts to support analysis, reflection, and research.

This standard, which builds on standard 8, asks kids to use evidence that supports analysis and reflection. This requires that your child determine his research focus and use sources that support this research focus. This standard requires that students narrow their focus to ensure the most relevant information is gathered for the research project. Students often need help with narrowing their research topics. You can assist your child with this by asking questions to help him narrow the focus. This involves collecting the most efficient resources to complete the research task. To help your child, continue to stress the importance of research, and provide opportunities for your child to conduct research for home or personal projects. Remind your child to think about his research topic and determine which resources will provide the necessary information to efficiently complete the research project. Helping your child learn how to effectively conduct research and find relevant information is a skill that will go a long way toward preparing him for success in college and the workplace.

CHAPTER 25

Expectations in 5th Grade Speaking, Listening, and Language

Fifth graders are expected to participate in group, one-on-one, and teacher-led discussions. This expectation is no different from those of the previous grade levels; however, in 5th grade students should be adequately prepared for the discussions and should have no trouble using appropriate behaviors and language for the given task. The speaking and listening standards in 5th grade also continue to build on the collaboration and active listening skills that students should already possess. The language standards focus on shifts in verb tense, proper use of commas and quotation marks, and using reference materials to help with spelling and vocabulary use. This chapter focuses on the skills that your child will be responsible for in the speaking, listening, and language standards of the Common Core.

Be Prepared

By 5th grade, students should be capable of adequately preparing for speaking and listening tasks. They should have read materials and have prepared adequate notes to use with their oral presentations. Speaking and Listening standard 1a reads:

> Come to discussions prepared, having read or studied material; explicitly draw on that preparation and other information known about the topic to explore ideas under discussion.

The standard clearly says that 5th graders should be well prepared for their speaking and listening tasks. You can support your child to meet this standard by ensuring your child has good notes and a good understanding of the topics being studied. Remember that by the 5th grade your child has been practicing public speaking for several years. In the 5th grade all of these skills come together so that your child can conduct well-rehearsed, engaging presentations.

Moving Discussions Forward

Students should be able to move discussions forward by asking appropriate questions that can help spark conversation and debate. Many students struggle with determining what they should say in order to help move the conversation forward without being redundant. This skill will require a lot of modeling. Students should be listening to debates on television or watching panel shows. These can be a starting point for determining what sort of language moves a discussion forward. Speaking and Listening standard 1c reads:

> Pose and respond to specific questions by making comments that contribute to the discussion and elaborate on the remarks of others.

By skillfully posing questions and responding in a way that encourages dialogue, your 5th grader can move discussions along, and more deeply delve into topics. Allowing your child to pose questions and discuss issues of importance is an effective way that you can help your child foster this skill.

Summarizing Information

Fifth graders need to be able to summarize information that is obtained from written, spoken, and digital sources. This standard was introduced in the 4th grade. Speaking and Listening standard 2 reads:

> Summarize a written text read aloud or information presented in diverse media and formats, including visually, quantitatively, and orally.

With this being the second year that this standard is in place, students should begin to demonstrate more independence for meeting it. Continue to encourage your child to summarize diverse information he finds in his readings, graphs, and other digital sources.

Clarifying Claims

Fifth graders are asked to identify the claims of a speaker and articulate how those claims are supported by reasons and evidence. Speaking and Listening standard 3 reads:

> Summarize the points a speaker makes and explain how each claim is supported by reasons and evidence.

In order to accomplish this task, your child must understand how to summarize claims and explain how they relate to specific reasons and evidence. Help support this task by asking your child to clarify or clearly state the claims he makes in his own work. Press him to give you specific reasons behind his claims. This exercise will help him understand his claims more clearly, which will enable him to articulate them better. This will also help him identify the claims of others so that he can ask for clarification as needed.

Presenting Information

Fifth graders should be comfortable presenting information in a professional manner. The use of technology and visuals should be utilized to enhance meaning.

Speaking and Listening standard 4 addresses this:

Report on a topic or text or present an opinion, sequencing ideas logically and using appropriate facts and relevant, descriptive details to support main ideas or themes; speak clearly at an understandable pace.

Speaking at an appropriate pace and using organized, relevant data is an important practice that 5th graders can master. You can support this by having your child practice her presentation before presenting it at school. This can help her clear up and revise any areas that need to be improved.

FACT

Taking the time to practice an oral presentation helps decrease anxiety. Studies have found that when students practice their oral presentations aloud they get higher scores, because they are more comfortable presenting.

Prepositions, Interjections, and Conjunctions

Fifth graders should be comfortable using conjunctions, prepositions, and interjections.

Prepositions

Prepositions link nouns, pronouns, and phrases to other words in a sentence. Prepositions come before a noun or pronoun to show that noun/pronoun's relationship to other words.

EXAMPLES OF PREPOSITIONS

- Example: I met the woman from Peru.
  - *From* links Peru to woman; and *the* tells you which woman.
- Example: We ran through the breezeway.
  - *Through* links breezeway to ran; and *through the breezeway* tells you where we ran.

Interjections

Interjections are words that express emotion. Interjections are separated grammatically from the rest of the sentence.

EXAMPLES OF INTERJECTIONS

- *Wow!* You did a great job.
- *Sure!* I will be there.
- *Well*, I would rather not go.
- *Oh*, I didn't know you wanted to come.

Using interjections when writing helps express emotion and makes writing vivid. Interjections are often used in poetry to convey the mood of the work.

Conjunctions

Conjunctions connect words or groups of words. Prepositions also connect words but, unlike prepositions, conjunctions don't have objects. Instead, they show a relationship between two words.

EXAMPLE OF A CONJUNCTION

- Are you going to Disneyland *or* Sea World?

Here is a list of conjunctions:

- And
- But
- Or
- Nor
- For
- So
- Yet

Understanding the proper use of conjunctions will help bring variety to sentences and will also help the writing become more interesting and easy to follow. Having your child pay attention to conjunctions as they are used in texts that she reads is a nice way to reinforce their use.

Verb Tense

Using the correct verb tense is another expectation for 5th graders. Language standards 1c and 1d read:

c. Use verb tense to convey various times, sequences, states, and conditions.
d. Recognize and correct inappropriate shifts in verb tense.

Verb tense can be a challenge for many students. Students may not realize that they switch from present to past tense in their writing or when speaking. As Americans, we have so many colloquial sayings and slang in our language that using the correct verb tense can be a challenge for some.

As the Language standard notes, students in 5th grade will be expected to demonstrate proper verb tense in their speaking and writing tasks.

Students need to be reminded that verbs tell us when things happen. Present, past, and future tense verbs should be used appropriately in writing. Your child will become aware that, when writing, it is important to use the same verb tense throughout the writing piece. Switching verb tense when speaking is commonplace in 5th grade. Students often switch tense, which can cause confusion for the listener. Remind your child to ensure he maintains consistent verb tense when writing and presenting. Making note cards is a good way for your child to record what he plans to say so he can avoid errors when the actual presentation occurs.

Verb tenses signify the time and place that action takes place. When students confuse and/or switch verb tense there is confusion about the timeline and sequence of events.

Presentations

As in 4th grade, 5th grade students are expected to present information in a logical manner with appropriate pacing and tone. Speaking and Listening standard 4 reads:

Report on a topic or text or present an opinion, sequencing ideas logically and using appropriate facts and relevant, descriptive details to support main ideas or themes; speak clearly at an understandable pace.

Appropriate pacing involves pausing when necessary and having a conversational style. Children are very familiar with appropriate pace and tone in reading. They have been reminded since kindergarten to read like they speak and not to read like a robot or a computer. This reading style is also a great way to help kids understand what appropriate pacing is when presenting.

Remind your child that, as she presents, she should use a conversational tone while paying appropriate attention to her language. Her goal should be to use a professional style and not use slang or other informal language.

Another aspect of 5th grade presentations is the use of multimedia to help enhance oral presentations. Speaking and Listening standard 5 reads:

Include multimedia components (e.g., graphics, sound) and visual displays in presentations when appropriate to enhance the development of main ideas or themes.

By 5th grade your child is expected to be comfortable using visual displays in her presentations. Visuals can be physical objects, or they can be digital objects created using computer programs like PowerPoint. Regardless, the important thing to remember is that the visuals must enhance the presentation and add value and meaning. The standard also notes that the multimedia components used should be appropriate. Sometimes students use audio or video clips that are not relevant to the topic. Helping your child think about the purpose of using a visual or audio clip will help her make informed decisions on what to include. Ask your child which types of visuals would help the listener understand the content better. Also, ask which types of visuals or charts would help organize the information being presented in a more effective way.

Support Activities

DIRECTIONS: CIRCLE THE WORD THAT IS SPELLED CORRECTLY. THEN WRITE THE CORRECTLY SPELLED WORD ON THE LINE.

1. acheing   aching   ayching   _____
2. explaining   explaynig   explaneing   _____
3. interesting   intresting   intristing   _____
4. stroling   strohling   strolling   _____
5. combeeng   combing   coaming   _____

DIRECTIONS: HAVE YOUR CHILD USE THE WORD BANK AND WRITE EACH DICTIONARY WORD NEXT TO THE CORRECT SET OF GUIDEWORDS.

Word Bank

car sweet hide tiger walk

1. **cape – crazy**   _____
2. **safety – swing**   _____
3. **have – home**   _____
4. **taste – two**   _____
5. **wait – west**   _____

DIRECTIONS: HAVE YOUR CHILD USE CONTEXT CLUES TO DETERMINE THE MEANING OF THE UNDERLINED WORD AND WRITE THE ANSWER ON THE LINES PROVIDED.

1. The large dinosaur statue was *immense*.
   Immense means

   _____

2. We ate an *appetizer* before the waiter brought our pizza.
   An *appetizer* is

   _____

3. The snow from the *blizzard* covered our cars.
   A *blizzard* is

   _____

4. I was exhausted and *weary* because we walked all day long.
   Weary means

   _____

5. The *radiant* sun shined brightly in the afternoon.
   Radiant means

   _____

DIRECTIONS: HAVE YOUR CHILD UNDERLINE THE PREPOSITIONAL PHRASE IN EACH SENTENCE.

1. The wind blew through the trees.
2. The boys jumped in the pool.
3. The baby crawled under the table.
4. Many planes fly over thunderstorms
5. We walked our dog around the neighborhood.

DIRECTIONS: HAVE YOUR CHILD USE THE WORD BANK AND WRITE THE PRONOUN THAT BEST COMPLETES EACH SENTENCE.

Word Bank
her they our his she

1. _____ curled her hair for the school dance.
2. He broke _____ video game.
3. My family lost _____ home in a fire.
4. _____ practiced for their soccer tournament all day.
5. Mom burnt _____ hand on the stove.

DIRECTIONS: HAVE YOUR CHILD REWRITE EACH SENTENCE WITH THE CORRECT PAST TENSE VERB. THE VERBS HAVE BEEN UNDERLINED FOR YOU.

1. The girls _runned_ quickly.

   _____

2. The dog _eated_ all his food.

   _____

3. We _was_ scared in the dark.

   _____

4. The picture _felled_ off the wall.

   _____

5. My brother _goed_ swimming with his friend.

   _____

CHAPTER 26

Bringing It All Together

The Common Core ELA State Standards provide students the opportunity to exit high school ready for the demands of college and the workplace. The skills emphasized by the Common Core standards are essential for allowing students to grow in the pivotal areas of literacy, including critical thinking, research, speaking and listening, and collaboration. These critical skills will help students think independently and work collaboratively to solve real-world problems. The K–5 ELA standards require students to begin thinking about creating arguments that are sound and have adequate support. They also require kids to learn to read and write in different genres. As these standards evolve and as we learn more about how to scaffold them to meet the needs of all learners, schools will continue to increase student learning by providing high expectations of rigor and accountability for all. As a parent, your role is to continue to gain information about the standards and stay in communication with the school regarding the changes and how they affect teaching practices.

Next Steps

At the time of this book's publication, students across the nation are being tested on these new standards. Soon it will be known how our students are faring, and decisions will be made regarding how to better teach these standards to help achieve mastery and success for all. As noted in Chapter 2 the Common Core standards have required instructional shifts or changes that have increased the level of rigor and the instructional materials and activities. This change will also be evident in the assessments students will take to show their mastery. As students continue through the elementary grade levels, they should be increasingly improving their ability to communicate, both in speaking and in writing. This will open doors for them to take on more complex material at the high school level and beyond. As a parent you should continue to inquire about the Common Core standards and provide opportunities for your child to engage in dialogue, read rich informational and fiction texts, and continue to provide opportunities for your child to practice his technology and keyboarding skills as he conducts research and writes. Schools will continue to provide training for their staff on how to best provide instruction using the Common Core standards. As we all grow and learn during this process, having parent support is pivotal to success.

FACT

States that have adopted the Common Core standards join an assessment consortia. The federal government provided grants to two assessment consortia to develop the assessments. They include Partnership for Assessment of Readiness for College and Careers (PARCC) and Smarter Balanced Assessment Consortium. Arizona and Florida have chosen American Institutes for Research (AIR) to develop their Common Core state assessments. For further information on the testing consortia check out the following websites: *www.air.org*, *www.smarterbalanced.org*, and *http://parcconline.org*.

Integrated Model of Learning

The Common Core standards advocate for an integrated approach to learning. The standards should be taught in relation to one another so that your child can see the connection between the various skills. Research has shown that when students can see a connection in what they are learning across content areas there is more learning and engagement. For example, this can be accomplished by teaching reading comprehension using a science text, and then having the child write about what she learned and follow up with an oral presentation. All of these experiences enrich learning and allow the child to gain a strong understanding of the content she is learning. By exposing your child to the content in various formats the learning becomes more solid and they have a deeper grasp of the concepts and become experts on the subject. Think about when you are learning a new skill. The more your engage in the learning in different contexts, the better grasp you gain. This concept holds true when children are learning. The more exposures they have to the content, the more skilled they become. That is the beauty of the integrated model of teaching.

Integrated versus Thematic Units

For many years teachers used thematic units to teach concepts. They may have taught a thematic unit about dinosaurs or the rain forest. Typically the classroom was immersed in an environment that emulated the theme. This may have included building a canopy to represent the rain forest, having books about the rain forest everywhere, and having worksheets that related to the rain forest. This is not what integration means for the Common Core. An integrated model requires that teachers teach related concepts across content areas. This may look like teaching kids about the importance of justice by having them read books with the theme of justice, having them write a letter to support a cause, and having them create a speech to discuss a justice matter. It is still the "thematic" concept, but the change comes in the level of rigor and relevance of the tasks children are asked to complete.

Workshops and Online Resources

One of the best ways to continue learning about the Common Core ELA standards is to connect with other parents online in workshops, blogs, and chats. There are numerous websites that provide information about the Common Core standards. You will find these resources a helpful place to go to learn how other parents are embracing the standards and additional resources that are available to use. Here are a few that give information for parents on what the standards entail and how to help support them at home.

- *www.corestandards.org/what-parents-should-know*
- *www.pta.org/parents/content.cfm?ItemNumber=2583*
- *www.engageny.org/parent-guides-to-the-common-core-standards*

Your local school district and public library are other resources to check for workshops on the Common Core standards. They provide opportunities to communicate with other parents about the standards and how to best help students succeed. Take advantage of these opportunities so that you can continue to build your knowledge of the standards.

FACT

Many parents are not sure where to find information to help support their understanding of the Common Core standards. Check with the following organizations that can provide guidance on avenues to acquire more information. The following website provides links to local parenting education organizations. Check to see what is available in your area: *http://npen.org/professional-development/ parenting-education-networks-organizations-and-programs-by-state.*

Talking to Your Child's Teacher

Your child's teacher will also be a great source of information on how the standards are being implemented in your child's classroom. Concerned teachers welcome parent input on the standards and skills they are teaching, and will provide supplemental strategies and support that parents can use at home with their children. The school year progresses quickly. To ensure you stay in touch with your child's progress throughout the year try keeping a calendar that reminds you of important dates to remember. Times of the year to note are the parent teacher conferences, testing dates, and school vacations. A few weeks before these dates is a great time to contact your child's teacher to touch base on her progress.

One thing to consider is to set up an initial meeting with your child's teacher to find out what you can do at home to support the standards. Don't wait until parent teacher conferences to initiate this dialogue. Begin the year by staying in touch with the teacher so you can be informed of any areas that you can begin supporting at home. Some questions to considering asking your child's teacher include:

- What can I do at home to help support my child with the Common Core standards?
- What books do you suggest I have my child read at home?
- How can I help improve my child's writing?
- What suggestions do you have for activities we can do at home to support what is happening in the classroom?
- What literacy strategies do you suggest I use at home?
- What are my child's strengths?
- What would you like to know about my child that would help you as the teacher?

These questions can help start a dialogue with your child's teacher as you work together to ensure success.

ESSENTIAL

Parent involvement is noted as one of the key factors in student success. Studies have found that academic achievement increases when parents are involved in their child's education. Consider joining your school's PTA or serving as a classroom volunteer. Both will provide opportunities to engage in your child's learning.

The Future of Common Core ELA State Standards

Recently, the Common Core standards have gained national attention, and proponents of the standards are strong. As with any new education initiative being informed and keeping abreast of new information will be key. At this time forty-three states and the District of Columbia have adopted the standards. Check out the map on the following website to see the status of states and their adoption of the Common Core standards: *www .corestandards.org/standards-in-your-state*.

Moving Forward

The information in this book serves as a resource that you can use to support the Common Core ELA standards with your K–5 child. The hope is that you will find ways to assist your child in building the skills and foundations she needs to be successful. The exercises that were included throughout the book provide an opportunity to engage in learning activities with your child. They serve only as a sample of the types of activities that your child may encounter in the classroom. The online games and resources included throughout the book provide engaging activities that your child can explore at home. Finally, use the tips and facts provided in each chapter to help answer any questions you may have about the standards. The websites included will prove a great source of information as you explore the standards. This is an exciting time as we learn about this new way of looking at education. The standards will help narrow a gap between what is taught from state to state and will help ensure kids are ready for the challenges in college and the workplace. Happy learning!

Glossary

accuracy
The ability for a student to recognize and/or decode words correctly when reading

active listening
The ability to listen, interpret, and exhibit an interest in what a speaker is saying

affix
A morpheme added to the base of a word to change the meaning

alliteration
Use of the same consonant at the beginning of each stressed syllable in a line of verse. The repetition of the initial sound(s) in neighboring words. Example: "Peter Piper picked a peck of pickled peppers."

anchor standards
The anchor standards, also referred to as the College and Career Readiness standards, are the general, cross-disciplinary literacy expectations that must be met for students to be prepared for college and the workplace.

author
A person who has written something, such as a book or another written piece

blending
Combing sounds represented by sounds/letters to read or pronounce a word

choral reading
Reading aloud together; a whole class or with a group of students

collaboration
The act of working together to accomplish a task

Common Core State Standards Initiative
Initiative of the National Governors Association Center for Best Practices and the Council of Chief State School Officers; the group developed a set of state-led standards. The standards define the knowledge and skills needed to be college and career ready. The standards were developed in collaboration with various stakeholders including teachers, school administrators, content experts, states, and parents. The goal of the initiative is to provide a curriculum that is rigorous so that students graduate from high school ready for college and career.

compound word
Two or more words are joined together to make them one word. Example: foot, ball, a football.

comprehension

The process of constructing meaning by using the author's words and reader's background knowledge

concepts of print

The understanding that print carries meaning, and that text contains letters, words, sentences, paragraphs, spaces, and illustrations. This also includes an understanding of the parts of books and the correct way to handle a book. For instance: front cover, back cover, reading from left to right and from top to bottom.

consonant

Speech sound that is characterized by stopping of the airflow to pronounce the sound; any letter except a, e, i, o, and u.

consonant blend

Two or more consecutive consonant letters at the beginning or end of a word that produce a distinct sound when the word is pronounced. Example: *str* in strange, *st* in trust.

consonant digraph

Two consonant letters that produce a single sound when a word is read. Examples: *th* in this, *ch* in chin, *sh* in wish, *ph* in phone.

context

The words that come before or after an unknown word that provide hints of the word's meaning

cooperative learning

Instructional strategy where groups of students work together to complete a task

cross-disciplinary

Instructional practices that go across content and discipline areas. For example, the ability to analyze information is important in math, science, social studies, and reading.

CVC word

Word consisting of a consonant-vowel-consonant pattern. Example: cat, man, sun.

decodable text

Text in which most words are comprised of previously taught letter sounds

decoding

Act of using letter-sound knowledge to convert written letters into spoken language

differentiated instruction

Offering learning experiences based on student need. Involves grouping students according to their individual needs. The teacher can differentiate reading by grouping kids with like skills needs in a small reading group. In that group, the kids would work on specific lessons to address their needs.

echo reading

Activity where students echo what was read or repeat the material as they track the words they are reading

editing
When writers proofread their writing to correct spelling, grammar, and punctuation errors

Elkonin boxes
Strategy that involves segmented letter sounds in a word by using boxes to represent each sound

environmental print
Signs, labels, and other print that are found in the community. Example: a stop sign, the name of a restaurant, a food label.

family literacy
Home and school partnership to help strengthen literacy development

fluency
The ability to read a text accurately, smoothly, quickly, and with expression. Fluent readers have better comprehension because they can read for understanding instead of putting so much energy into decoding the text.

graphic organizer
A visual or pictorial way to express knowledge and concepts. Example: a Venn diagram or a story map.

illustrator
The individual/artist who illustrates a book

informational text
Text that is used to communicate factual information. Example: dictionary, nonfiction texts, cookbooks, news articles.

invented spelling
An attempt by beginning writers to spell unknown words by using sounds that they know or any other prior knowledge

Language standards
Reading standards related to teaching grammar, vocabulary, and conventions

letter sound correspondence
Knowledge that the letters of the alphabet represent sounds

letters
In English, twenty-six letters, each being represented by an upper- and lowercase letter; e.g., A (uppercase), a (lowercase)

lexicon
Words used in language by a person or group of people

Lexile levels
Information used to indicate an individual's reading ability or the difficulty of a text. The Lexile level is shown as a number with an "L" after it—700L is 700 Lexile.

manipulatives
Objects used to help a child grasp a learning concept. They are used to provide an

opportunity for hands-on learning. Manipulatives include blocks, shapes, letters, small toys, etc.

monosyllabic
A word that has one syllable, such as "big" or "man"

narrative texts
Texts that are fictional in nature, including poetry, drama, and fiction

oral reading fluency (ORF)
The ability to read, speak, or write fluently. Can be measured by the number of words read per minute using a reading passage.

partner reading
Activity where a student reads aloud with a partner(s); may be used to practice reading fluency

phoneme blending
The ability to identify a word when hearing parts of the word in isolation

phoneme isolation
The ability to isolate a single sound within a word

phoneme manipulation
The ability to change or move the individual sounds in a word

phoneme matching
The ability to identify words that have the same beginning sound

phoneme segmentation
The ability to break words down into individual sounds

phonemic awareness
The ability to hear and manipulate individual sounds (phonemes) in words

phonics
Method of teaching reading with a focus on the phonetic makeup of words. Phonics teaches the relationship between letters and individual sounds of spoken language.

phonological awareness
The skill that includes identifying and manipulating units of sound in oral language, including words, syllables, and onsets and rimes

prefix
An affix attached to the front of a word to add to or change the meaning

print awareness
Growing recognition of conventions and characteristics of written language: punctuation, capitalization, directionality in reading (left to right, top to bottom in English), the spaces between words marking word boundaries, how print in the form of words corresponds to speech

prosody
Reading with expression, and appropriate tone. Prosody involves reading with a rhythmic tone with intonation.

publishing
Final copy of writing that has been edited and ready to share with an audience

quick write
Activity where students are given a limited timeframe to write about a topic

r-controlled vowel
When a vowel is followed by an R, and the R changes the sound. Example: bird, word, farm.

rate
How quickly and accurately a person reads

Reading: Foundational Skills standards
Reading standards that relate to teaching reading concepts of print, alphabetic principle, phonics

Reading: Informational Text standards
Reading standards that relate to factual texts including how-to manuals, cookbooks, nonfiction texts, biographies, etc.

Reading: Literature standards
Reading standards that relate to poetry, drama, and fiction

Reading Recovery
A reading program developed by Marie Clay. It is a short-term, intensive, one-to-one intervention program for 1st grade students having difficulty with reading.

revising
Step in the writing process when writer makes changes to his writing to clarify meaning

rhyme
One of two words or phrases that end with the same or similar sound. Example: cat/sat, stamp/ramp.

sight words
High-frequency words that children are encouraged to memorize. Example: the, said, she, this.

Speaking and Listening standards
Standards related to developing oral language and interpersonal skills

suffix
An affix added to the end of a word or stem

syllable
A single unit of a spoken or written word that has an uninterrupted sound

title page
The page at the front of a book that provides information about the title, author, publisher, and place of publication

vowel team
Two vowels that are side by side and create a new sound. Example: boil, goat, fruit.

word family

Group of words that have a common feature or pattern. Example: "at" word family includes the words cat, hat, mat, pat, and sat.

word segmentation (syllable segmentation)

The ability to identify the components of a word or phrase

Writing standards

Standards related to writing, including writing argument/opinion, narratives, and informative/explanatory text

Short and Long Vowel Sounds

SHORT VOWEL SOUNDS				
A a	**E e**	**I i**	**O o**	**U u**
apple	elephant	igloo	octopus	umbrella
cat	egg	pig	box	sun
LONG VOWEL SOUNDS				
A a	**E e**	**I i**	**O o**	**U u**
ape	eagle	ice	ocean	unicorn
cake	bee	pie	boat	cube

Index